TURN OFF THE DARKNESS

CHANGING YOUR WORLD
FOR GOOD

DAVID CERULLO

TURN OFF THE DARKNESS

Scripture quotations are from the
NEW KING JAMES VERSION of the Bible.
Copyright © 1979, 1980, 1982,
Thomas Nelson, Inc., Publishers.

Scriptures marked KJV are from
The Holy Bible, KING JAMES VERSION.

Published by
The Inspirational Networks
9700 Southern Pine Blvd.
Charlotte, NC 28273

ISBN: 1-888-7600-15-9

Printed in the United States of America.

DEDICATION

This book is lovingly dedicated:

− to my parents, Morris and Theresa Cerullo, who throughout my life have guided me by word and example. They instilled within me a spiritual foundation and heritage for which I will be forever grateful.

− to my wife, Barbara. My closest companion, best friend, and love of my life.

− to our two adult children, Ben and Becky. A wonderful example of the faithfulness of God. No parent could be more proud of their children. They are both truly a heritage from the Lord.

− to families everywhere battling against the forces of darkness. May this book help you protect yourself and those you love. You can turn off the darkness. You can win the battle of life!

3

CONTENTS

INTRODUCTION

This book is not for the casual reader. On these pages you will come face to face with uncomfortable issues that are striking at the heart of our nation – and assaulting our homes.

It is an understatement that the media has become a powerful and pervasive force in our world. At the forefront of the media barrage is television, making an indelible impact on our society. Without question it shapes and molds the minds and hearts of all who watch – for good or bad.

Perhaps more than any other single ingredient, television has torn at the very fabric of our culture, negatively influencing the attitudes, values, beliefs and even the behavior of millions. In the process our families, and our children – yours and mine – have suffered.

Since the founding of our nation, great leaders have repeatedly proclaimed that *when we lose our moral compass, we lose our way.* Now, that compass is giving an uncertain reading.

When there is no longer a basis for right or wrong, then truth becomes what seems right or wrong at the moment.

"Truth" becomes subjective, interpreted differently by each person. The result has been devastating – and the impact of this onslaught has been painfully clear. Many families and children have been torn apart through divorce, drug abuse, teen pregnancy, crime, abortion, and so much more.

It is rare to find a family that has not been affected in some way as a result of these negative influences inflicted on our society.

What is the source of this darkness? Where does it come from? The Apostle Paul told the believers at Ephesus, "For we do not wrestle against flesh and blood, but against principalities, against powers, against the rulers of the darkness of this age, against spiritual hosts of wickedness in the heavenly places" (Ephesians 6:12).

As we will discuss, we are spiritually at war. This is an epic battle for the souls of your children, your family and your loved ones.

THE BATTLE LINES

What are our choices? We can sit back and do nothing, complaining about how bad things are:

- how morally bankrupt television, movies, music and videos have become.
- how we have to constantly monitor and review what we allow our children to hear, watch, and read.
- how much of a negative impact television is having in our daily lives.
- how much the Internet is bringing pornography

and questionable content into our homes.

Or, we can do something about it.

The battle lines must be drawn, and we cannot avoid asking the question: *Am I willing to declare war?*

We must not take the easy road and simply declare war on the symptoms. The Word declares that "the kingdom of heaven suffers violence, and the violent take it by force" (Matthew 11:12).

In this conflict that is raging for the souls of our families, I, for one, say it is time we become spiritually violent. This means being aggressive, forceful, and pro-active.

Because you are reading this book, I believe you are one of those who desires to do something positive. I feel you want to see not only a drastic change, but a *Christ-centered* change.

TOLERANCE AND ACCEPTANCE?

For too long Christians have tolerated the negative influence of the media that is penetrating our society – our families, our children.

Edmund Burke, the 18th century English politician, said: "The only thing necessary for the triumph of evil is for good men to do nothing." It is true of nations, and true in our homes.

Where does transformation begin? With one person, one child, one family.

Most lasting change comes about slowly. After all, the world did not get into this tragic state overnight. Our values did not erode quickly. So-called "politically correctness" did not just appear out of thin air.

We need to realize that *what the world calls political correctness is almost never morally correct.* Yet society asks us not only to be *tolerant,* but to *accept* every form of deviance. We are being told, "Be inclusive, not exclusive." And "Don't offend anyone."

This philosophy is just one more deception and lie the enemy has perpetrated against us. God's Word commands that we speak the *truth* in love (Ephesians 4:15). Unfortunately that truth *is* going to offend people.

Scripture tells us that the Gospel is "a stone of stumbling and a rock of offense" to those who are disobedient, but "precious" to those who believe (1 Peter 2:7-8).

As I write these words, the emphasis of The Inspirational Networks' ministry is on television and the Internet. Someday the Lord may lead us into the development of film and motion pictures or even music. But, in large part the focus of our ministry is helping to change lives through television. We continually ask, "How can God use television through us to help change lives?"

SOLVING THE PUZZLE

I believe we can help *change the world for good.* I often think about the pastor who was at his desk preparing his Sunday sermon. He wife came in and asked if he could watch their young son while she ran an important errand. Even though he was busy, he agreed.

Naturally, the little boy wanted to play with his dad, yet this just was not the time. The dad thought to himself, "What can I do to keep my son occupied while I finish this message?"

Looking around his study, he noticed a stack of magazines. He picked one up and began to thumb through the pages. An idea struck him as he came across a large advertisement for a multinational company that included a map of the world.

The dad called his boy over and said, "I have a challenge for you. Do you see this picture of the world? I am going to cut it up in little pieces and make a puzzle out of it. I would like you to put it back together. When you do, I have a special reward for you."

Well, off went the pastor's son. Within minutes, there was a knock on his door – standing there was his boy with the map of the world. It was all back together, neatly glued down on a piece of paper.

The pastor was amazed. "Son," he said, "how were you able to put the puzzle together so quickly?"

The boy replied, "Well dad, I really did not know where all the countries and continents went, but as you were cutting it up I noticed that on the *other* side was an advertisement for men's clothes, with a picture of a man. When I saw that, I said to myself, 'All I need to do is to put the man together right and then the world will be right.'"

The pastor smiled, told his boy what a great job he did, and gave him the reward he promised. He said, "Son, you have just given me my message for Sunday. If we can get the man right, we can get the world right."

It is still true. If we are ever going to repair our world we are first going to have to start with man. We must begin one person at a time.

HOW WILL THEY HEAR?

To make a difference through television, I am convinced it is important to produce two distinct kinds of programs. The first attempts to share the gospel and *evangelize* people. The second type of program has a focus to *disciple* people, to "equip the saints" as Paul referred to in Ephesians 4:12.

Many churches and various ministries are effective in producing "traditional Christian programs." What is missing are efforts directed towards reaching the lost and meeting their needs.

In the Word we are asked: "How then shall they call on Him in whom they have not believed? And how shall they believe in Him of whom they have not heard? And how shall they hear without a preacher? And how shall they preach unless they are sent?" (Romans 10:14-15).

In terms of television, I also ask, "How will they hear if they won't watch – or aren't watching?"

From personal experience, most people know that television programming must be relevant, compelling, entertaining, informative, and engaging. Programs that do not pass these tests are rarely watched, even by Christians. That is why I believe it is essential for the Body of Christ to produce programs that will broaden the scope of those who watch Christian television today. Most important, we must be certain that our "evangelistic" outreach is redeeming in its message.

THE VISION

Long ago, through the prophet Joel, God said, "And it shall come to pass afterward That I will pour out My Spirit on all flesh; Your sons and your daughters shall prophesy, Your old men shall dream dreams, Your young men shall see visions" (Joel 2:28).

God has given me a vision:

- A vision to redefine what Christian television is.
- A vision to create programming that will make a difference in people's lives.
- A vision to help get the man right and therefore get the world right.
- A vision to reach people with the Gospel through television – those who would not ordinarily watch Christian programs.
- A vision to change the world – your world – for good, one life at a time through this unique medium.

God told Habakkuk to "Write the vision, And make it plain on tablets, That he may run who reads it. For the vision is yet for an appointed time; But at the end it will speak, and it will not lie. Though it tarries, wait for it; Because it will surely come, It will not tarry" (Habakkuk 2:2-3).

13

The primary reason for this book is to write the vision and make it clear so people like you have an opportunity to share what God had laid on my heart. I also hope, and pray, that this book will help you see what you can do in your own area of influence.

RAISING A STANDARD

You may be unfamiliar with The Inspirational Networks. As of this writing, The Inspirational Networks are comprised of three networks: The Inspirational Network (INSP), Inspirational Life (I-LIFE), and Inspirational Education (INSP-E).

The Inspirational Networks are cable and direct-to-home satellite-delivered television networks dedicated to reaching this generation with the gospel through media. We are committed to being channels you can trust, places you can turn to find hope, encouragement, and a word from the Lord. We are pleased we can present many different churches and ministries proclaiming the Gospel, bringing strength to the body of Christ. We are also dedicated to producing original, entertaining, informative, motivational, wholesome, value-based, Christ-centered, life-enriching, life-changing, inspirational and redemptive programs for you, and your entire family. We are unwavering in our commitment to help you take back what the devil has stolen from your children, families, marriages, finances and physical bodies.

Scripture declares, "Where there is no vision, the people perish" (Proverbs 29:18). I believe the reverse is equally true, *without a people, the vision will perish.* You are an indispensable part of the "people" who can make this a reality.

It is my prayer that this book will give you an insight to the influences that surround us – and also challenge you to do everything possible to protect yourself and those you love against the spiritual forces waging war against you and your family. You will learn how you can take charge of your own home against this onslaught.

I believe you recognize that it is time we raised a righteous standard and allow God to use us – *together* – through the media to make a difference in our world.

– David Cerullo

CHAPTER ONE

WHO'S KILLING OUR KIDS?

Eric Harris and Dylan Klebold, their minds filled with hatred and their coats bulging with explosives, walked into Columbine High School in Littleton, Colorado, in April of 1999, and unleashed a bloody rampage that shocked the world. When the massacre was over, fifteen people were taken to the Denver morgue.

"Why?" asked troubled parents and perplexed psychologists. "What has gone wrong?" wondered confused clergy and anxious educators. Media pundits seemed to have more questions than answers:

"Can we solve the problems by taking away guns?" some speculated.

"Do we put pressure on Hollywood writers and producers?"

"Is the profit motive of the media the culprit?"

"Should parents be blamed?"

"What about the impact of violent computer games, music lyrics, and MTV?"

"Where is the clear voice of the church?"

These questions echoed the same kinds of questions that had been raised in the preceding months as other teens acted with similar violence:

- Kip Kinkel, a high school freshman, shot both his parents and opened fire on fellow students in Springfield, Oregon.
- Sixteen-year-old Luke Woodham went on a shooting spree at his school in Pearl, Mississippi.
- While students were finishing an informal prayer meeting Michael Carneal, fourteen, shot eight fellow students at his Paducah, Kentucky, high school.
- Drew Golden and Mitchell Johnson killed four students and a teacher in Jonesboro, Arkansas.

AN ADDICTION

As president of a television network whose programs reach millions of homes every day, I am deeply concerned about what is happening to the young people of our nation. The evidence seems to be clear that teen violence is the outward signal of a much deeper crisis that threatens the foundation of society. Everywhere, people are searching for solutions. The answers, in part, can be seen by examining the images that are portrayed in the media today. According to the American Psychological Association, "The average child in our nation has seen 8,000 televised murders and 100,000 acts of violence by the end of elementary school and has watched about 22,000 hours of TV and some 18,000 murders in the media by the end of high school."[1]

Some young people have become simply hooked. A high school junior confessed, "Television is an addiction and I am an addict."

CAUSE AND EFFECT

Adding to the debate over the media's influence in society, the American Academy of Pediatrics reported in 1999 that "Every day, thirteen American children and adolescents die in gun-related homicides, suicides and accidents. Many more suffer permanent injuries."[2]

> A HIGH SCHOOL JUNIOR CONFESSED, "TELEVISION IS AN ADDICTION AND I AM AN ADDICT."

In a major study of television violence, L. Rowel Huesmann and Leonard Eron of the University of Illinois, surveyed every eight-year old in a typical American city in 1960. They conducted follow-up studies with the same subjects in 1971, 1981 and 1994. The results were startling. "The correlation between violence-viewing at age eight and how aggressive the individual was at 19 was higher than the correlation between watching violence at age eight and behaving aggressively at age eight," says Eron. He estimates that television is responsible for ten percent of the violent behavior in this country. "But if we could reduce violence by ten percent, that would be a great achievement." [3]

These facts invite the inevitable question: Is there truly a cause-effect relationship between what people watch on television and what they act out in real life? Can the disturbing statistics be blamed on the motion picture and television industry?

According to U.S. Senator Orrin Hatch, "Exposure to media portrayals of violence increases aggressive behavior in children." And he added, "As one expert put it, arguing against the link between media violence and the violent actions of our youth is 'like arguing against gravity.'"[4]

> "THE EFFECT OF MEDIA VIOLENCE ON OUR CHILDREN IS NO LONGER OPEN TO DEBATE."

A 1999 report from the U.S. Senate Judiciary Committee states, "The effect of media violence on our children is no longer open to debate."[5] The document concluded that what dominates children's lives is "exceedingly violent'" and that such images lead to acted-out violence.

Noted critic Michael Medved agrees. He says, "A wealth of scientific studies in recent years have removed most of the remaining doubts about the link between make-believe brutality and real world aggression."[6]

THE INTRUDER

Television is by far the most influential medium our society has ever known. It shapes standards, sets trends and monopolizes time. Unfortunately, in many lives it has become more of an *intruder* and less of a *guest*. Rather than being a source of inspiration, uplifting entertainment, and education, it is being blamed for many of the ills that plague our culture.

You can find people in the media elite who disagree with this assessment, yet most people know it is true. The vast majority of Americans believe television contributes to social problems such as violence, divorce, extramarital sex, teen pregnancy, and the decline of family values.

Ask any educator about the effective learning techniques and they will tell you that visual input is far more powerful than reading or listening. When you add the repetitive nature of television, the images are being permanently etched on our minds.

Katherine Montgomery, president of the Center for Media Education, says, "The accumulation over time is the concern, not a single incident or a single viewing. A steady diet of violent content over time creates a culture that tells kids that violence is the accepted way we solve our problems."[7]

THE "GOOD GUYS"

The messages sent by programs that focus on murder, rape, and man's inhumanity to man is presented in the worst possible light. Much of television glamorizes the negative

– immorality, lustful behavior, licentiousness, and even evil. The "good guys" – people who are attractive role models – frequently are the ones who commit violent acts. And often there is no remorse, criticism or punishment. To make matters worse, the violence is often accompanied by humor.

Rarely do programs focus on the harm caused to the victim's family and friends. We are seldom told of the devastation brought about by offensive acts.

Because of the shocking headlines involving students being killed in schools there have been demands by leading voices in our society that violent acts in the media must be significantly decreased. Yet when you look at prime-time programming on most television, little has changed. In fact, a report by the Parents Television Council in August 1999 revealed that "The content of the family hour (8-9 P.M.) overall is becoming more lewd and crude than ever."[8]

We, at The Inspirational Network (INSP), have conducted studies in many cities across America through a market research technique called "Focus Groups." In these situations, a professional market researcher and communicator comes into a room of ten to twelve people to ask a series of questions. The people have been pre-selected and screened based on a variety of criteria they match. They are representative of a target audience we are attempting to reach.

In these focus groups we have heard people state their dissatisfaction with viewing choices. Here is a sample of the comments they shared:

"Television networks aren't providing us with the

kinds of programs we really want to watch."

"We want to see more uplifting, worthwhile programs."

"We are fed up with what we're seeing on television. There is too much garbage!"

"Who is producing this kind of stuff?"

"What makes them think this is the kind of television we want to watch?"

> ## "WE ARE FED UP WITH WHAT WE'RE SEEING ON TELEVISION. THERE IS TOO MUCH GARBAGE!"

It has been said that "something is better than nothing." In the case of some network programming, *nothing* is better than this!

LETHAL LYRICS

Television is not the only source of violence. Our young people are being bombarded with troubling messages in the lyrics of hit songs and images of music videos.

Thomas Storke, Professor of Communications at Stanford University said at a government hearing, "Both heavy metal and rap present many disturbing images of violence and sex. Such content occurs in anywhere from 25% to 70% of metal and rap songs and/or videos."[9]

Storke also reported on a study finding that "heavy metal music tends to be the almost unanimous choice of drug involving youth." And he reported a case study which determined that "eliminating access to MTV decreased the frequency of violent acts among teenagers and young adults in a locked treatment facility."

Additional research at Wake Forest University sampled over 500 music videos and found that 25% of all videos aired on MTV contained "weapon-carrying" images: "holding a knife, gun, club, whip, chain, rope, or other weapon (or) actual use of a weapon."[10]

In the music videos of groups such as Guns-N-Roses and Beastie Boys, there are as many as 36 scenes of violence in just one song.[11]

What is happening in our homes? Often the parents do not really know. According to the Child Care Bureau of the U.S. Department of Health and Human Services, nearly five million school-age children spend time as latchkey kids without adult supervision during a typical week.

> # NEARLY FIVE MILLION SCHOOL-AGE CHILDREN SPEND TIME AS LATCHKEY KIDS WITHOUT ADULT SUPERVISION DURING A TYPICAL WEEK

"Child's Play"

It is impossible to calculate the harm to society because of the television programs children are watching or the films they slip into a VCR with parents looking the other way.

In Manchester, England, four young people confessed to murdering a teenage girl. While the killing was in progress, one teen spoke a line from the film *Child's Play* – a movie in which a demonic toy named "Chucky" terrorizes his victims. Not long after that incident two ten-year-olds from Liverpool were found guilty of killing a two-year-old they had lured away from his mother at a shopping mall. Perhaps you remember the story. It was curious that the father of one of the boys had recently rented the sequel to *Child's Play*, titled *Child's Play 3*.

It is not difficult to agree that society has a major problem, yet few can offer a solution.

What is the answer to the dilemma we face?

- Must government take action?
- Are the networks and Hollywood to blame?
- Would public outrage solve the problem?
- What is the role of parents?
- Do our children need more media education?

As you will discover, these are only partial answers to the puzzle.

CHAPTER TWO

THE DEATH OF VALUES

The United States is one of the most religious nations in the industrialized world, in terms of level of stated religious beliefs and practices. According to the Gallup Organization, "Virtually all Americans attest to their faith in God and approximately half of the population attends a religious service every week."[1]

Consistently, studies show that 95 percent of our citizens believe in God and more than 80 percent agree that "religious values should play a role in everyday decisions."[2]

Despite this strong central core of belief, our society increasingly has been drifting away from our common heritage and value structure. In years past few would have believed this drift could have been possible. Yet it has taken place before our eyes – subtly and steadily.

Surveys also report that most Americans believe religion is losing its influence on American life and that values in our society have been seriously declining.

I have attended countless conferences, meetings, and other public and private forums involving business leaders in this country and am continually amazed at how few people really care about values – about eternal things or making a difference in the world. Our Judeo-Christian value systems based on the Bible has gone from being the cornerstone of society to something many people are trying to explain away, ignore, or willingly violate. They want us to *abandon* it – to bury it!

A prominent television executive from one of the top four networks was recently quoted as saying, "Family programming is absolutely worthless."

What a sad perception of the American family. Think of it! They are saying "You are worthless!"

This moral deterioration is becoming obvious in our schools, businesses, communities, families, and even churches. I am especially aware of the problem in the arena of television.

MOCKED MERCILESSLY

In many ways it is hard to believe that the media elite in the country could be so out of touch with the principles that most Americans hold dear. Yet that is exactly what has happened.

It seems that one of the surest ways to guarantee becoming the object of derision by comedians and the target of scorn from writers, commentators, and even some politicians, is to take a stand for values.

I am sure you can still remember when former Vice President, Dan Quayle, was mocked mercilessly for suggesting that the television program, *Murphy Brown*, was wrong when it celebrated – and even promoted – sexual promiscuity. He championed the importance of values, family, and the sanctity of marriage.

While still a U.S. Senator, Bob Dole criticized record companies, film studios, and others, for promoting lyrics, themes, and products that encouraged violence, rape, hostility toward police and other authority figures. He too became a subject of derision as critics accused him of threatening censorship.

You only have to listen to a few talk shows and the comments of comedians and commentators to understand that the vast majority in the media blast anyone who dares to suggest that there should be *any* standards – or that some things are morally wrong.

> ## THE VAST MAJORITY IN THE MEDIA BLAST ANYONE WHO DARES SUGGEST THAT THERE SHOULD BE ANY STANDARDS – OR THAT SOME THINGS ARE MORALLY WRONG

Most Americans agree with our criticisms. Surveys show

that roughly two-thirds of adults feel television has a detrimental effect on the family and that TV in general portrays negative values, yet they continue to turn on the darkness and do nothing to institute change.

THE MORAL DECLINE

The overwhelming number of Americans also believe that television shows do not represent their own personal values.

> # THE OVERWHELMING NUMBER OF AMERICANS BELIEVE THAT TELEVISION SHOWS DO NOT REPRESENT THEIR OWN PERSONAL VALUES

Consistently, surveys conducted for *Newsweek, Associated Press, Time/CNN,* the *Los Angeles Times,* and others, report that the majority of adults believe there is too much violence on television.

A report by the Parents Television Council (PTC) in May 1999 concluded that offensive contact on television has actually increased, even though a ratings system has been initiated to help police content. L. Brent Bozell, PTC's chairman, concluded that the ratings system has "backfired because some irresponsible members of the entertainment industry would see the

30

opportunity presented by the ratings system to insert even edgier content into their shows."[3]

Widespread concern over violence and offensive programming caused Congress in 1995 to mandate the installation of a V-chip for greater parental control of viewing.

The Gallup Organization reports that 67 percent are dissatisfied with the ethics and moral standards of the American people and over 70 percent are unhappy with honesty and standards of behavior of people today.[4]

When asked, "Do we need to return to traditional values?" the vast majority of citizens continue to say "Yes!"

People still long for the day of "a kinder, gentler nation" – without the road rage, without drive-by shootings, without teens being killed on campuses.

However, the question is always asked, "What do you mean by values?"

In past generations, one could always point to rock-solid covenants such as the Ten Commandments. Surely people can agree to them. Well, it is no longer the case. Some individuals are uncomfortable with *any* reference to moral influence, or even something as basic as the Ten Commandments.

Why was this democracy founded? Our forefathers came to America in search of religious freedom. Our pledge of allegiance underscores this in reciting "one nation under God." These great men and women wanted to express their Christian principles without government interference. Oh, how far we have drifted!

You cannot imagine how advertising agencies, television

networks, program producers, writers, and others, seem to recoil almost in horror at the suggestion that they agree on some kind of moral code. You can often sense their repulsion at being linked with any form of religion.

Describing Values

One of the most useful studies on this topic in recent years was conducted by the Massachusetts Mutual Insurance Company.[5]

In their survey of 1,050 adults, the following conditions are the percent who said that these statements describe family values "very well."

- Being able to provide emotional support to your family. 85%
- Respecting one's parents. 85%
- Respecting one's children. 85%
- Being responsible for your actions. 83%
- Respecting others for who they are. 78%
- Taking care of your parents in their old age. 77%
- Being able to communicate your feelings to your family. 74%
- Leaving the world to the next generation in better shape than we found it. 70%
- Having faith in God. 69%
- Being married to the same person for life. 68%
- Following a strict moral code. 61%
- Being married. 60%

- Having children. 56%
- Helping your community or neighborhood. 50%
- Earning a good living. 50%

These conditions provide a consensus definition of *family values* that are clear to most people, and to which most can agree.

THE COMMANDMENTS

Using these commonly-held beliefs as a reference point, we have created our own *Ten Commandments of Family Values*. We believe in the importance and truth as represented in:

I   A vital relationship with God, and a responsibility to God, community, and oneself.

II   Morality and a life based on Biblical values.

III   Respect for others and the sanctity of life.

IV   Caring for others.

V   Faith in God.

VI.   Improving life for oneself and others.

VII.   The institution and ideals of marriage.

VIII   Children and the importance of enhancing their future and role in society.

IX   Financial responsibility and accountability.

X   Getting along with others.

It would be significant if every major television and

movie producer, network and distributor could agree to these commandments.

THE NUCLEAR FAMILY

The days of Ozzie and Harriet Nelson and Ward and June Cleaver seem linked to the ancient past. The *Brady Bunch* was basically a story of growing up in a home where love and virtue were everyday standards.

Television shows were built around what has been termed the "nuclear" family – mom, dad, sister and brother – all living under one roof.

Without advance notice, the '80s and '90s ushered in a twisted picture of the family. Millions were watching *Married with Children* and *The Simpsons* – programs that derided the notion of responsible living and respect for others. *Ellen* and *Will & Grace* taught today's generation that anything goes between women and women and men and men.

> WHAT IS "HARMLESS ENTERTAINMENT" DOING TO THE STRUCTURE OF THE AMERICAN FAMILY?

I shudder to think at the ripple effect from the recent network season where seventeen of the characters in prime-time programs were homosexual. What is this so-called "harmless entertainment" doing to the structure of the

34

American family?

Arguably, the definition of *family* is changing.

According to one study, more singles – and women in particular – believe it is unlikely they will find a suitable marriage partner. Unfortunately, many choose the option of out-of-wedlock motherhood. From 1976 to 1995, the percentage of high school girls who said it may be worth it to have a child out of wedlock rose from 33 percent to 53 percent.

Cohabitation has become increasingly popular. In 1960 fewer than half a million American couples lived together out of marriage. Today, over *four million* couples think it is a convenient way to keep from being lonely, to save some money, or to try out a relationship before getting married.

I believe it is vital for us to return to an understanding that the family unit has been the bedrock, the foundation, the heart and strength of our society. If we do not have stable family units how can we have a strong nation?

The understanding and definition of a "family unit" must begin in the home, and based upon a Biblical definition – not with what the world attempts to define or label as a family.

We must deliver a wake-up call to society. It is time we stopped caving into pressure groups who want us to compromise what we believe is morally right for our nation and our families. They want public *tolerance* and *acceptance* – more than that, they want us to *embrace* what the Bible calls *sin*.

When did every form of sexual deviance stop being a sin or crime – and become accepted as "an alternative lifestyle?" When did God change His mind and decide to sanction and approve what He had previously called an abomination?

We're Desensitized

Drugs, alcohol, and violence against women have been glamorized by the entertainment industry. Listen to the lyrics of rap music and you will be appalled.

It is estimated that 13 million Americans over the age of twelve are users of illicit drugs. And we know that usage can start much earlier. This scourge is costing society $70 billion every year for health care, auto accidents, extra law enforcement, crime and lost job productivity.

In addition to drugs, 14 million abuse alcohol – and over four million admit to being "binge" drinkers.

In our nation there is a woman beaten every one to three minutes and a woman is raped every two to five minutes.

> ONE OF THE GREAT DANGERS OF WHAT IS HAPPENING IN OUR CULTURE IS THAT WE ARE BECOMING DESENSITIZED

One of the great dangers of what is happening in our culture is that we are becoming desensitized. Young people are numb to the violence they see and hear depicted in music and videos. They see a kid "shoot up" in a movie and it no longer wrenches their emotions. They watch as a young woman is sexually exploited and it does not stir their anger. It is *more* than tragic for society. It is a cancer that is eating away at our culture and trying to destroy our very souls.

Many have seen so much, so often, that their conscience has been seared. They are in danger of being turned over to a "reprobate mind" (Romans 1:28).

We have allowed these things to happen so frequently that we have become calloused.

Have you ever had a callous? What once was sore and sensitive becomes so hardened that we no longer feel it. We see it, yet it no longer bothers us.

What we view on the average day can make us numb. We see sin, sex, violence with such repetition we say, "Oh, we can take it or leave it."

We are lulled into saying, "I don't need to change the channel because this scene – this little snippet I find offensive to my values and beliefs – is going to be over in a minute. If I just stick with it, this will pass and I can watch the rest of my program." We have been lulled into a pit of darkness.

> MANY HAVE ENTERED INTO SUCH A COMFORT ZONE THAT IT IS MORE CONVENIENT TO IGNORE THE PROBLEM

Many have entered into such a comfort zone that it is more convenient to ignore the problem. Often, parents turn a blind eye to what their children are absorbing, not willing to remove the offense, the sin, the darkness – they willingly allow the callous to develop.

It takes work to stay sensitive. We are admonished: "Do not be conformed to this world, but be transformed by the renewing of your mind, that you may prove what is that good and acceptable and perfect will of God" (Romans 12:2).

Our minds and hearts are analogous to a garden. What we allow ourselves to watch, listen to, think on, are the seeds that take root and grow.

However, the garden of our life and spirit must be tended. We need to pull the weeds, condition the soil, plant the right seeds and provide adequate water and nourishment.

WHAT KIND OF SPIRITUAL AND EMOTIONAL GARDEN ARE YOU CULTIVATING?

What kind of garden are you expecting to grow? If we allow negative, dark and destructive seeds to be planted, why are we surprised at the results?

If you constantly watch programs filled with hate, anger, bitterness, violence, crime, verbal abuse, substance abuse and sexual permissiveness, what kind of spiritual and emotional garden are you cultivating? What do you expect to reap?

WHAT HAPPENED TO FAITH?

The constant barrage of secular values in society is taking

its toll. The 1999 Gallup Report on "The Spiritual Life of Young Americans,"[6] found that "a deep religious faith" ranks only eighth out of nine values stated as being *very important* among our youth.

- 92% say it is very important to have peace and happiness.
- 91% say it is very important to be well educated.
- 66% say it is very important to help people in the community.
- 60% say it is very important to get married some day.
- 52% say it is very important to have children.
- 44% say it is very important to have lots of money.
- 43% believe it is very important to have a deep religious faith (33% say it is somewhat important. 23% believe religious faith is not very important).
- 16% say it is very important to have fame.

It is also interesting that 29% of teens report that they have personally experienced the presence of God in some manner. And 67% say they have never felt they were in the presence of God.

IT IS TIME TO RETURN

America has been steered in the wrong direction. We

must return to values on three levels:

1. Biblical values.

Our values must be based on the uncompromised Word of God. In many ways, they are the principles of truth, nobility, purity and love found in Philippians 4:8.

Biblical values will cause us to have a renewed burden for souls. They challenge people to fulfill the Great Commission. The Bible transforms us by the "renewing of our minds" and the "washing of the Word." It moves us to take on the nature of Christ. "Therefore if any man be in Christ, he is a new creature: old things are passed away; behold, all things are become new" (2 Corinthians 5:17).

2. Patriotic values.

We need to continually uphold a love for our nation. I am not talking about blind patriotism, but a celebration of those values that bind us together as a people – our heritage, tradition, history, and common bond. This encourages a love of community and actions that build strong relationships in our cities. Patriotic values stimulate us to care for the less fortunate, to reach out to the sick, homeless, and helpless.

3. Traditional family values.

We need to champion those ideals that uphold the fabric of our society and sustain our most precious relationships – the sanctity of marriage, the bond linking parents and children, the care and respect for older generations.

I may be naive to think this, but I feel we can once again

have a society in which these values are encouraged and embraced. It is my hope and prayer.

A MODEL TO FOLLOW

One of the great men in the Old Testament is Joseph, the son of Jacob. He has become one of many role models for me. Joseph took a stand in a hostile culture.

He was not a perfect man. Yet God loved him and placed a call on his life.

God gave Joseph a dream and a vision. Because of that, his brothers despised him. They were jealous of the favor that their father showed Joseph over themselves. In their jealousy and contempt, they sold Joseph into slavery in Egypt – although he had done nothing that deserved such judgment. Scripture records that, even in Egypt, he steadfastly focused on doing what was right, although he had no encouragement.

Joseph showed patience and persistence, not giving up despite years as a slave – confined to prison for doing nothing wrong. He continued to persevere, serving God. He continued to hold onto the dream and vision that God had given him.

> JOSEPH IS A MODEL MANY CHRISTIANS WOULD DO WELL TO ADOPT

He had no clue that all this time, the Lord was working on his behalf – in his family, with the world, and in his

41

own life.

Eventually God brought to pass the fulfillment of the dream and vision that He had given Joseph. God exalted Joseph – at the right time. He emerged from prison to become ruler of all Egypt, the most powerful nation in the world. He came forth to fulfill his destiny.

Joseph is a model many Christians would do well to adopt. Too often we allow the enemy to bring circumstances into our lives that cause us to lose sight of the dreams, visions and destiny that God has planned for us. Do not allow that to happen.

Instead of complaining about your circumstances, move forward with character and integrity and allow God to work through you in your world. Do not become discouraged or resigned to defeat. If you do, the devil will use your circumstances to defeat *you*. Keep your eyes on the dream and on God. He will bring it to pass. The Bible says that God is not a man that he should lie. Has he not spoken it? Will he not perform it? (Numbers 23:19).

A SPIRITUAL EARTHQUAKE

Paul wrote to the Galatians, "Let us not grow weary while doing good, for in due season we shall reap if we do not lose heart" (Galatians 6:9-10).

These are problems Paul experienced firsthand. He knew the persecution that came from serving God.

In Philippi, Paul cast a demon from a slave girl. "But when her masters saw that their hope of profit was gone, they seized Paul and Silas and dragged them into the marketplace to the authorities" (Acts 16:19).

The local business interests seemed to have won the day when Paul and his companion, Silas, were thrown into prison – for doing something noteworthy.

By their actions, the standards of the authorities were set. They were more interested in maintaining profit motives and placating business leaders than they were in setting people free from sin and bondage.

Paul easily could have been discouraged and given up. Instead, he committed himself to the Lord and filled the jail with praise and worship.

How did God move on their behalf? He sent an earthquake that not only set Paul and Silas free, but led to a revival in Philippi.

Today we need an earth-shaking of at least 6.8 on the *spiritual* Richter scale. People are in bondage and need to be set free. Far too many of God's people are confined to mental, emotional and financial prison cells. These walls need to come tumbling down!

We must boldly proclaim the gospel and reestablish Biblical values beginning in our individual lives, then in our families and finally in our nation and the world as Christ intended.

CHAPTER THREE

STRANGLEHOLD ON SOCIETY

The founders of our nation were wise. They devised a plan for representative government where the leaders of our nation – the ones who make laws – would be elected directly from the people. No self-appointed dictators. No inherited positions.

The same cannot be said for those who have far more influence over the culture of our nation – those who bear the title "Media Elite."

Who are these clever writers, creative directors and enterprising producers who each year deliver thousands of hours filled with humor and drama? Are they "the people next door?" Are they "one of us?"

Far from it.

A *Public Opinion* survey of 104 of the most influential leaders of television's creative community revealed that there were "45 percent who claim no religious affiliation whatsoever" and 93 percent who say they seldom or never attend religious services."[1]

Does that sound like an accurate representation of America?

In a 1992 study, professors from the University of Dayton, Duke University Medical Center and Northwestern University examined more than 100 productions on the major networks. They looked for religious content and images and here's what they found. Only 5.4 percent of the characters had an identifiable religious affiliation – even though 89 percent of Americans attest to belonging to an organized faith.[2]

While providing a representative form of government, our Founding Fathers also provided for freedom of speech and freedom of the press. These are important safeguards and establish the basis upon which we have the liberty to preach the gospel through the media.

Those in the Media Elite operate under the principles of freedom of speech and freedom of the press. They also have a right to hold their views.

However, many within this Elite have used these freedoms to project *their personal* views on the families of America. Their opinions and lifestyles, which are often out-of-step with the beliefs of most Americans, are often treated as "normal" and "accepted." Thus freedom of speech has become a justification for license, irresponsibility, and unrestrained expression.

God's people need to wake up. We have choices. We do not have to allow these people to control what we see in our homes. The answer is for Christians to "turn off the darkness" and stop the influence of these people in our families. We need to let the Media Elite know that we will no longer watch programs that encourage standards that violate Biblical principles. We want programs that uphold and support our beliefs and values, not ridicule them. Then we need to "light a candle" so there are viable alternatives.

DISTORTING THE FACTS

> ## WE NEED TO LET THE MEDIA ELITE KNOW THAT WE WILL NO LONGER WATCH PROGRAMS THAT ENCOURAGE STANDARDS THAT VIOLATE BIBLICAL PRINCIPLES

The term "Judeo-Christian" has been used for decades as an inclusive concept to satisfy the largest possible population. No more. Because of the rise of Mulsim, Buddhist and Hindu groups in our nation, the media tries to stay far away from espousing any religious principle. Of course, targeting fundamental Christians in the name of comedy is fair game!

Tim LaHaye, in his book *The Hidden Censors,* states that the forces of secular humanism control the media. "An ideological monopoly exists," he observes, "comprised of people who are unsympathetic and often hostile to the traditional values held by most Americans. In the entertainment media, they glorify moral degradation. In the news media, they distort the facts so that they conform to their view of 'reality.' In the name of freedom, they assault us with a barrage of liberal biases, socialistic ideals and relativistic values – and suppress religious, conservative, and pro-moral expression."[3]

ONLY A REFLECTION?

For years we have listened to program producers and network executives deflect the notion they are responsible for shaping and influencing young minds. They continue to shrug their shoulders and argue, "We merely create entertainment that reflects the culture."

Hollywood, television and the media can bury their head in the sand all they want. The truth is that in our communities, kids are acting out what they see. The moral and physical damage to society is real.

Few would argue the fact that *The Jerry Springer Show* lowers the civility standard of television, yet for years stations have stood in line for his program. Why? High ratings – which drives up advertising revenue.

The constant barrage of these daytime talk shows has made perversion seem normal.

The World Wrestling Federation (WWF) has been soundly chastised for its overt sexual innuendo, violent story-lines and incivility. Yet the audience cannot seem to get enough – and young children are watching by the millions.

THE DOUBLE STANDARD

It is appalling to witness the double standard of the Media Elite regarding such programming. In public they scold. In private they smile.

When one network executive was criticized for carrying a wrestling series that features blatant sexism and excessive violence, he retorted, "These are classic stories of good and evil."

> IN PUBLIC THEY SCOLD. IN PRIVATE THEY SMILE.

Television and magazines have made heros out of men and women who champion ungodly lifestyles – including Dennis Rodman of the NBA, shock-jock Howard Stern and singer Madonna. MTV has elevated Beavis and Butthead, two animated characters who ridicule anything Godly, righteous and worthwhile.

DECISIONS IN DARKNESS

The Media Elite did not grow up saying, "I am going to Hollywood, and when I arrive, I'm going to tear down the standards of our country. I am going to celebrate violence and malign religion."

No. These decision makers in the entertainment capitols

are basically a product of their environment, making most choices based on either greed or profit.

We need to understand that their entire value system is different from yours and mine. How can a person expect to see when they walk in darkness and have no light? Many of these talented people have relatively no concept that the story lines for the programs they are producing are heavily influenced by forces of darkness.

> # How Can a Person Expect to See When They Walk in Darkness and Have No Light?

LOWERING THE BAR

Somewhere, a broadcast executive had to make the decision to begin a format known as "Tabloid News." It is a prime example of how the bar of morality has been lowered in our culture.

According to a study by the Center for Media and Public Affairs (CMPA), stories about sex, crime, drugs and alcohol drive the leading syndicated tabloid TV news programs. "The shows rarely criticize the titillating sexual behavior they report on," the study found, "despite being watched by large numbers of children."[4]

Here's what CMPA researchers learned after analyzing 333 reports that appeared during two weeks of programming on *Inside Edition, Hard Copy, Extra, Entertainment Tonight, American Journal* and *Access Hollywood.*

- 24% of all stories dealt with crime.
- 21% dealt with sex.
- 17% dealt with accidents and disasters.
- 10% focused on self-destructive behavior such as drug and alcohol abuse.
- Only 7% dealt with "uplifting" themes such as heroic acts.

Leading the sexual topics was extramarital sex with 29 reports. Other stories centered on pornography and homosexuality. It was noted that "fewer than one in five reports (10%) on sexual activity contained any criticism." And homosexuality was never criticized.

The startling fact of this report revealed that these shows "average a combined audience of nearly two and one half million children, the majority of them between two and eleven years of age, according to Nielsen ratings."

It is a sad day for our country when social deviance is masqueraded as news.

THE 30-SECOND TEST

When I hear producers of unwholesome programs say, "It's just entertainment, it has absolutely no influence on the values or behavior of society," I am dumfounded.

How can anyone really believe that? Why in the world

do major advertisers spend billions of dollars each year buying thirty second commercials – in an attempt to influence something as significant as our buying habits – if television does not really impact our behavior?

The fact is that advertisers spend these enormous amounts on television precisely because they believe that the message contained in their 30-second television spot is powerful enough to attract millions of people to purchase a product. Do they believe the media can change or influence behavior? Absolutely!

> # DO THEY BELIEVE THE MEDIA CAN CHANGE OR INFLUENCE BEHAVIOR? ABSOLUTELY!

If people's buying habits can be affected in seconds, just think what kind of influence is made on a person's values, beliefs and behavior in a thirty-minute or one-hour television production, or a two-hour motion picture?

If the celebrities of Hollywood and New York are simply actors and entertainers with no underlying motives, then why do they so frequently champion causes from AIDS to saving animals? As noted media critic Michael Medved observes, "These industry leaders take great pride in the positive plugs for condom use, or saving the rain forests, that they've been able to insert in even the most incongruous contexts on television, in movies and in popular songs."[5]

He continues. "Such efforts highlight the schizophrenic attitude of show business professionals toward the larger significance of what they do. On the one hand, they believe that they can influence the audience on behalf of worthy causes like safe sex and recycling; on the other hand, they continue to insist that violence, hedonism and selfishness often featured in their work will have no real-world consequences whatever."

IN THE CROSSFIRE

Most media corporations are public companies with pressure to generate profits. Perhaps that is why the word "value" has an economic rather than a moral connotation.

Rupert Murdoch, one of the most powerful and influential people on the world scene in communications talks about his conservative beliefs and strong family-values bias. Yet in business, his FOX television network was built on irreverent programming that frequently ridiculed Biblical principles. *Married with Children* is a classic example.

In many ways the public is caught in the crossfire between industry moguls who are involved in personal rivalries. Their only focus is on

> IN MANY WAYS THE PUBLIC IS CAUGHT IN THE CROSSFIRE

winning – yet they are making moves that impact lives. The programs involved set the standards and tone of life today.

What should be our attitude toward the media elite?

We need to realize these men and women are not gods incarnate. They are people like you and me who have somehow arrived at their destination with an opinion far different from ours.

They were influenced regarding their current beliefs and they can be persuaded to change.

WAKING UP

While television, movie and music executives cling to their charted course, the American people are slowly beginning to open their eyes. We are waking up.

> THE AMERICAN PEOPLE ARE SLOWLY BEGINNING TO OPEN THEIR EYES. WE ARE WAKING UP.

Let me turn again to Michael Medved, who says, "Few of us view show business as a magical source of uplifting entertainment, romantic inspiration, or even harmless fun. Instead, tens of millions of Americans now see the entertainment industry as an all-powerful enemy, an alien force that assaults our most cherished values and corrupts our children. The dream factory has become the poison factory."[6]

IS THERE HOPE?

Before you conclude that the film and television industry is beyond hope, let me tell you about a meeting I had in Hollywood. It was arranged by my friend, Ted Baehr, a long-time film executive.

Seated around the table were talented writers, producers, directors and other executives from major West Coast studios – each a committed Christian. The discussion centered on the potential for producing quality Biblically-based films and television programs.

These men told me some of their frustrations. Many were disturbed by the environment in which they worked. They were bothered by the kinds of compromises and choices they felt compelled to make.

To a man, they stated they were hungry to work on films and television programs based on Biblical principles, and uphold family values. And they said that they knew of other talented people in Hollywood who shared their commitment.

What was needed, they commented, were networks, production companies, sponsors, and others with resources and a commitment to produce these programs. "Where *are* the people who really want programs based on Biblical principles? What are they doing to provide an alternative?"

They looked at me, and, to my amazement, asked *me* to help *them*. I asked these men what I could do. After all, the resources of our organization are small compared to those of the media giants in Hollywood. But I said I would do what I could.

55

I SAW THAT GOD HAS PEOPLE IN PLACE — READY TO PRODUCE THE *RIGHT* KIND OF PROGRAMS

That day I saw another vision. I saw that God has people in place – ready to produce the *right* kind of programs. Just as Jesus had said, "The harvest truly is plentiful, but the laborers are few. Therefore pray the Lord of the harvest to send out laborers into His harvest" (Matthew 9:37-38).

I resolved then and there to try to seek more laborers, and pray that God would raise up men and women, and companies, who would take the resources and talents that God has given them so we could go together into the harvest fields of our world.

Ted Baehr is one example. Ted has been a tireless champion of the need for morality to pervade our entertainment. He has lobbied studio and network executives and has been a real liaison between the Christian market and the media.

Fifteen years ago Ted Baehr established MovieGuide,[7] a popular rating system that gives families the confidence to know that the motion pictures they choose to see will be uplifting to their families. Every reviewed film is coded to indicate violence, sex, nudity, alcohol, drugs and much more. For example, the film's worldview is rated B-Biblical, C-Christian, E-Environmentalist, H-Humanist or Social, Ho-Homosexual, FR-False Religion, NA-New Age, etc.

Today we need more men and women like Ted Baehr who are willing to take a stand and place commitment to Christ above profit, position and job security.

Pray for our media leaders – that they will turn their hearts toward God.

CHAPTER FOUR

"BE CAREFUL LITTLE EYES"

In Dallas, a three-year-old died as a result of a "clothes line" wrestling move inflicted during play by the boy's seven-year-old brother.[1]

At first, Dallas Police and officials at Children's Medical Center believed that an adult must have caused the severe head injuries sustained by the preschooler.

When the brother was interviewed by police – as his sibling hovered near death – he showed the officers exactly what happened. They held a doll the size of a three-year-old as the older brother rushed at it with his arms straight out at shoulder level. He struck the doll in the neck, knocking it to the floor.

It was a move he had seen on television – watching pro wrestling.

Sadly, the little boy died a short while later from brain swelling.

ACCEPTANCE, IMITATION

> ON AVERAGE,
> KIDS ARE
> SPENDING
> NEARLY THREE
> HOURS A DAY
> IN FRONT OF
> THE TELEVISION
> SCREEN

In a world where prime-time television serves up such violence, how can we avoid reaping what has been sown?

On average, kids are spending nearly three hours a day in front of the television screen – and for some, *seven* hours is not unusual. When you add weekend viewing, many are spending more time watching TV than they spend in a school classroom.

What happens to children when they are exposed to television violence? Here is the conclusion reached in dozens of studies:

- They become immune to the horror of murder, rape and other violent acts.
- Gradually, they accept it as a way to resolve situations.
- They imitate what they see on television.
- They identify with certain characters – both victims and aggressors.

Research, statistics and data can often sound cold and

impersonal. Yet how would we respond if a member of *our* family were targeted by someone intent on committing a vicious copy-cat act. What if the bullets from a drive-by shooting were flying through *your* window pane?

What if your son or daughter became so absorbed by a story line that they projected themselves into the script?

> # WHAT IF THE BULLETS FROM A DRIVE-BY SHOOTING WERE FLYING THROUGH *YOUR* WINDOW PANE?

JUST A GAME?

The potentially damaging input is not limited to television. Many child experts are alarmed at the content of video games.

Dr. William Cockburn, a clinical pediatrics instructor, says, "Some of these games are so violent, so graphic, so filled with detrimental content, that simply going to the local toy store and picking up what Jack and Jill has put on their wish list without any pre-screening or research might prove dangerous."[2]

Parents need to thoroughly evaluate a game's potential impact on their child before purchasing any video game. Review it personally – and never allow your child to become preoccupied with this form of entertainment.

THE IMPACT

The response of a child to what they watch on television may vary, yet the danger is always present.

"THE IMPACT OF TV VIOLENCE MAY BE IMMEDIATELY EVIDENT IN THE CHILD'S BEHAVIOR, OR MAY SURFACE YEARS LATER."

According to the American Academy of Child and Adolescent Psychiatry, "Extensive viewing of television violence by children causes greater aggressiveness. And sometimes, watching a single violent program can increase aggressiveness. Children who view shows in which violence is very realistic, frequently repeated or unpunished, are more likely to imitate what they see. The impact of TV violence may be immediately evident in the child's behavior, or may surface years later, and young people can be affected when the family atmosphere shows no tendency toward violence."[3]

For children of very young ages, some experts are saying they should avoid television altogether.

In a 1999 report released by the American Academy of Pediatrics, "Children under two shouldn't watch television at all, not even 'Barney' or 'Sesame Street.'"[4]

The report stated that "research shows direct interaction

with parents and other caregivers is necessary for babies' and toddlers' healthy brain growth and the development of social, emotional and cognitive skills. Watching television may interfere with that interaction."

AN INNOCENT SCREEN?

The box we placed in the corner of our room has grown. It is no longer an innocent screen with colorful pictures. Now, along with information and entertainment, it fills our atmosphere with filth and garbage – making invisible scars on the lives of our children.

We are so fascinated, so mesmerized by the images, we refuse to close our eyes or pull the plug.

> IT FILLS OUR ATMOSPHERE WITH FILTH AND GARBAGE – MAKING INVISIBLE SCARS ON THE LIVES OF OUR CHILDREN

Like the frog who sat in a pot of water that was being slowly heated to a boil on the stove – "I like this . . . this is nice," he smiled. "It's warm." The water came to a boil so slowly that the frog did not feel the change in temperature until it was *too late.*

At first it is just a little humor that makes us blush. Then we get so used to the language that, unconsciously, we find the same words creeping into our vocabulary.

Little by little Satan has used television to encroach upon our lives. We watch program after program, hour after hour, until the seeds of darkness and destruction have been planted into our life and spirit. Suddenly, the fruit of those seeds manifests itself in our lives. Without knowing what happened, we find ourselves with a new set of values, beliefs, behavior and, yes, with a different relationship to God. We have allowed ourselves to be exposed to sin to such an extent that like Samson, we have become bound, blind and a servant to darkness.

> # WITHOUT KNOWING WHAT HAPPENED, WE FIND OURSELVES WITH A NEW SET OF VALUES, BELIEFS, BEHAVIOR

THE "SOAPS"

It is beyond my comprehension why a mother would allow her seven or eight year old daughter to watch the "Soaps" every morning during summer vacation. Just one review of the story line should be enough for a parent to say, "We do not need this in our home."

"Soaps" are based on torrid love affairs and illicit relationships. Yet look at the ratings – and the voyeurism.

Millions of women project themselves into these offensive plots. Why? Because they are fulfilling the lust of the flesh.

Now, in the name of entertainment, they are encouraging their daughters to follow their example.

"WHY CAN'T I?"

Somehow, the words of that song we learned in Sunday School need to echo in our mind. "Be careful little eyes what you see . . . Be careful little ears what you hear."

When my wife, Barbara, and I were raising our two children we put those words into practice – carefully screening what our family watched. We wanted to know where Ben and Becky were, who they were with, what they were watching, reading and listening to.

I can still remember them protesting, "Why can't I watch it? Everybody at school does." And more than once they argued, "Why can't I go? All my friends will be there!"

As parents we could not be responsible for the actions of others, yet we were accountable to God for how we raised our family. The directive in Scripture is clear: "Train up a child in the way he should go, and when he is old, he will not depart from it" (Proverbs 22:6).

> MORE THAN ONCE THEY ARGUED, "WHY CAN'T I GO? ALL MY FRIENDS WILL BE THERE!"

"AS FOR ME"

We must take seriously what we will permit to enter our lives – and the lives of our children through our eyes and our ears. And when that choice is made we should declare it.

When the children of Israel crossed the Jordan over into the promised land, they put up twelve stones, one for each of the tribes and made a large pillar. God spoke through Joshua and said, "These stones shall be for a memorial to the children of Israel forever" (Joshua 4:7).

What was the point? They were saying, "As for me and my house, we will serve the Lord" (Joshua 24:15).

> DOZENS OF TIMES EACH DAY WE MAKE CHOICES REGARDING WHAT WILL OR *WILL NOT* BE PART OF OUR LIVES

Dozens of times each day we make choices regarding what will or *will not* be part of our lives. We must have the spiritual fortitude to declare, "I am not going to allow that into our home."

God has given us the discernment to know right from wrong. He expects us to take charge of the environment of our home.

We must set boundaries regarding:
- places we will go.
- things we will do.

– what we will listen to.

– what we will watch.

There must also be places we will *not* go, things we will *not* do, things we will *not* listen to and things we will *not* watch.

Will you lead the way?

CHAPTER FIVE

THE BATTLE
FOR YOUR SOUL

B efore we can understand the forces that are tearing our world apart we must recognize two basic principles:

> *First:* Man lives in two separate worlds – a
> *natural* world and a *spiritual* world.
> *Second:* There are only two powers at work in the
> universe: God and Satan.

We have been discussing how the media has negatively affected human behavior, yet these are only physical manifestations of a spiritual problem. In the unseen world there is a battle being fought that dwarfs any conflict recorded in history. It is the conflict between good and evil.

Why have we seen such a major erosion of our values, beliefs and behavior during the past few decades? Millions of people have chosen rebellion over righteousness and disobedience over a firm decision to live by God's commandments.

Satan has influenced the minds, will, emotions and attitudes of people to disobey God, selecting their own destructive path instead of surrendering their heart and will to the lordship of Jesus Christ.

> # WE HAVE BECOME THE "IF IT FEELS GOOD, DO IT" GENERATION

We have lost our direction by walking away from God's Word – the guidebook and manual that reveals our Heavenly Father, His nature and character, and that shows us how to live in harmony and right relationship with Him – and therefore with our fellow man. Many have believed a lie and allowed our world to become one of "relativism," where almost nothing is absolute. We have become the "if it feels good, do it" generation.

Either the Bible is God's Word and divinely inspired or it is not. Either it shows us who God is, what His plan is for us and how we should live – or it does not.

The psalmist declared, "Thy word have I hid in my heart that I might not sin against thee" (Psalm 119:11).

RULERS OF DARKNESS

What does Scripture tell us concerning the battle that is underway? "For we do not wrestle against flesh and blood, but against principalities, against powers, against the rulers of the darkness of this age, against spiritual hosts of wickedness in the heavenly places" (Ephesians 6:12).

What are these principalities? What are these powers? Who are the "rulers of the darkness of this age" and the "spiritual hosts of wickedness in the heavenly places?"

From the beginning of time, this conflict for the soul of man has been bitterly fought.

When God created man and woman in the Garden, He desired fellowship and companionship. Immediately, Satan, in the form of a serpent, began to drive a wedge between the Creator and His creation, Adam and Eve.

The only rule given by God was: "Of every tree of the garden you may freely eat; but of the tree of the knowledge of good and evil you shall not eat, for in the day that you eat of it you shall surely die" (Genesis 2:16-17).

Satan, the tempter, lied to Eve, convincing her that God did not mean what He said. He told her, "You will not surely die" (Genesis 3:4).

Today, the devil is still perpetuating his lies. He is seductively whispering in the ears of millions: "Go ahead and *watch* – it won't harm you. Eat, drink and be merry – you only live once!"

> TODAY, THE DEVIL IS STILL PERPETUATING HIS LIES

Many have been "weighed in the balances and found wanting" (Daniel 5:27).

SUPERNATURAL STRENGTH

We need to unmask Satan for who he is: the adversary of the Almighty and the enemy of our soul. He has never stopped his campaign of deceit and destruction.

I remember when I was a young boy hearing my dad preach on the story of Samson and Delilah. You probably remember the story of Samson from Sunday School. God had a special covenant relationship with Samson and a plan for his life. Samson was to be a judge and a ruler. Because of divine favor, he was given supernatural strength to fight against and defeat the enemies of God's people.

As a direct result of temptation and sin, Samson was deceived by Delilah and lost more than his strength – "he did not know that the Lord had departed from him" (Judges 16:20).

Samson not only lost his power and his relationship with the Lord – and God's presence in his life – he lost his dream and his destiny. He forsook being the man God intended him to be, and forfeited the plan the Lord had for his future.

The Philistines took him away, blinded him – bound him – tied him to a grinding wheel and made him their slave.

At the end Samson called out to the Lord for forgiveness. Yet even though God restored his strength and his relationship with God, his life was required. His dream and destiny was forfeited.

BOUND AND BLIND

What is the ultimate penalty of sin? Death.

72

Those are the same consequences of sin in our lives. Look again at what happened to Samson.

The first thing the Philistines did to Samson was to *bind* him. He could not escape. That is what sin does in our lives. It binds us and there is no way out, no escape.

Then the Philistines put out his eyes. They *blinded* him. That is the next thing that the devil through sin does in our lives – blinds us. Sin blinds us to the truth. It blinds us to God's plan, purposes, dreams, visions and destiny for us.

Then the Philistines made Samson their slave. They tied him to a grinding wheel and made him grind grain. This is the consequence of sin in everyone's life. Sin makes us its slave.

> FOR A MOMENT OF PLEASURE, HE MADE THE WRONG DECISION

Finally, sin brings forth its ultimate conclusion – spiritual destruction and death.

Remember, Samson had a choice. He could either obey the Lord or not. For a moment of pleasure, he made the wrong decision.

We must make the right choices. We must choose life over death.

"I WILL PASS OVER YOU"

In Egypt, when the children of Israel were suffering great persecution, God told Moses that He was going to "pass through the land of Egypt . . . and will strike all the firstborn . . . against all the gods of Egypt I will execute judgment: I am the Lord" (Exodus 12:12).

He gave Moses specific instructions that resulted in the Passover. A lamb "without blemish" was to be sacrificed, and some of the blood of the lamb was to be placed on "the two doorposts and on the lintel of the houses" (Exodus 12:5,7). God said, "And when I see the blood, I will pass over you" (v.13).

Moses announced that "the Lord will pass through to strike the Egyptians; and when He sees the blood on the lintel and on the two doorposts, the Lord will pass over the door and not allow the destroyer to come into your houses to strike you" (Exodus 12:23).

The Bible says that in the fullness of time God sent forth His Son, "slain from the foundation of the world" (Revelation 13:8).

The Passover was a foreshadow of Christ, who was offered as a sacrifice for sin. John the Baptist said, "Behold! The Lamb of God who takes away the sin of the world!" (John 1:29).

Christ's death on the cross was God's plan for redemption. Only through His shed blood is there cleansing from sin.

ONLY ONE CHOICE

Who will you serve? God or Satan? There are many who may ask, "Why do I have to make a choice? I'm a good person. Just because I do not accept Christ does not mean I am serving Satan."

Unfortunately, it does. There is no "in-between" – no gray area. You are either a child of God, or a child of Satan.

Your choice is clear. You can accept the sacrifice of God's only son, Jesus Christ, or believe the lies of the devil.

We can never change our world for good unless we

> ## YOU ARE EITHER A CHILD OF GOD, OR A CHILD OF SATAN

have personally experienced the transformation of a new birth. "For all have sinned and fall short of the glory of God" (Romans 3:23). Scripture declares that "the wages of sin is death, but the gift of God is eternal life in Christ Jesus our Lord" (Romans 6:23).

If you do not already, you can know the joy of having your sins forgiven by accepting Jesus Christ as God's sacrifice. His shed blood on Calvary paid the price of redeeming you from the curse of sin and death. Jesus Christ purchased your salvation with His shed blood on Calvary and justified you – "just as if" you had never sinned.

Regardless of the iniquity that abounds in our world, God never banishes anyone to hell. We are given the opportunity to either accept or reject Christ as our Savior. Our eternal consequences are a result of our choice.

Jesus declared, "The thief does not come except to steal, and to kill, and to destroy. I have come that they may have life, and that they may have it more abundantly" (John 10:10).

A NEW START

Right now, you can know that your sins have been forgiven – that your relationship with the Father has been restored. All you need to do is ask Jesus Christ to come into your heart and be the Lord of your life.

Pray these words from your heart:

> *Dear Jesus. I admit I am a sinner and confess my sins to you. By faith I ask you to come into my heart. Cleanse me from sin with Your precious blood. Be the Lord of my life. Thank You, Lord, for saving my soul. Thank You for saving me now. In Jesus' name I pray. Amen.*

God, by His grace, will give you a new beginning. "Therefore, if anyone is in Christ, he is a new creation; old things have passed away; behold, all things have become new" (2 Corinthians 5:17).

You will be transformed! No matter what your sin, He promises to remove your sins "as far as the east is from the west, so far has He removed our transgressions from us" (Psalms 103:12).

Will trials and temptation cease? No. Will life suddenly be made perfect? No. The spiritual battle will still rage – and perhaps even increase since Satan will test your new-found

THE BATTLE FOR YOUR SOUL

faith. Yet you can say with Paul the Apostle, "O wretched man that I am! Who will deliver me from this body of death? I thank God; through Jesus Christ our Lord!" (Romans 7:24-25).

By choosing Christ over Satan, you can declare victory over the battle for your soul.

CHAPTER SIX

DECLARING WAR ON DARKNESS

I have come to hate this life," wrote Mark Barton in Atlanta in July, 1999, before taking the lives of his wife, and two beautiful children. "I have come to have no hope. I don't plan to live very much longer . . . just long enough to kill as many of the people that greedily sought my destruction."

Next, in a desperate rampage, Barton stormed through two investment offices, killing nine people and wounding thirteen others. Then he turned the gun on himself.

The tragedy shocked the nation. But this was only one of a series of senseless acts of violence that have become all too common in recent times. In fact, the Associated Press noted that there had been *at least ten major multiple shootings* in the United States in the first eight months of 1999, including the killings at Columbine High school near Littleton, Colorado.[1]

At a memorial service for Barton's victims, Atlanta mayor Bill Campbell stated, "No one, including our innocent children, is immune from the evil of violence."

> ## "No One, Including Our Innocent Children, Is Immune From the Evil of Violence."

Yet, even in the face of such tragedies, it seems that surprisingly little is being done to stop the "evil of violence" from infecting the hearts and minds of our families.

The violence in 1999 prompted a public outcry. Congressmen and community activists stood on their soapboxes with loud rhetoric demanding a reduction in violence. Some said the easy access to weapons was a primary cause. Others wanted to strengthen school security. Many pointed their finger at the entertainment industry and insisted that Hollywood clean up its act.

While this furor occupied the nation's attention, very little was being done to make a concrete change. One of the reasons is that most people have a very short attention span. Events that inspire deep emotions are soon forgotten. All it takes is a hurricane, earthquake, important political event, or other action of significance to change our national conversation.

And darkness and evil continue their onslaught. Can anything be done to stop this invasion? Or is it hopeless?

THE CAUSE

All of us know how easy it is to be caught up in causes. Often inspired by a tragedy, or watershed event, the public's attention can be galvanized. Violence is one of those issues that attracts a wide spectrum of interest and enthusiasm. At least for a short time.

> ALL OF US KNOW HOW EASY IT IS TO BE CAUGHT UP IN CAUSES

Responding to concerns expressed by outraged citizens, many within the television industry recognized that violence in the media needed to be addressed.

I have watched, and even participated in this debate.

As president of a cable television organization, I have been privileged to be part of this dynamic communications industry. I have made many wonderful friends, and discovered that many people throughout cable are genuinely concerned about providing a quality service, protecting the lives of the families in their communities, and want to provide an outlet for the gospel in homes across America.

We at INSP have tried to make a difference by participating in industry events and organizations. Our staff of dedicated professionals is respected by cable systems and other networks. In fact, many on our INSP staff have come to us from these organizations and have maintained solid relationships.

We are still trying to make a difference, from within the industry, and as part of it.

Yet at times I am troubled by some of the things that go on in our industry. And, frankly, I am concerned by the lack of concrete action that has taken place to address the issue of violence.

One recent focus has been to encourage the adoption of a ratings system for television programs. When they asked us to put these ratings on our network, we simply have said that all of our programs are rated "G."

> ## "PRIME TIME SEX AND VIOLENCE ACTUALLY HAD INCREASED IN SPITE OF THIS VOLUNTARY RATING SYSTEM."

Yet to us, this effort seemed to be hypocritical. The reality is that this system does not stop the offensive programming. It may do some good, with some people, but it has done nothing to halt the flow of sex and violence.

In fact, a study the Parents Television Council released in May 1999 reported that prime time sex and violence *actually had increased* in spite of this voluntary ratings system.[2]

This was only one of many attempts by the industry to pay attention to this problem. One of the most visible attempts was a campaign called "Voices against Violence," launched in March 1995. The campaign had been developed over a period of more than a year of planning by key network and cable system operators.

JUST A REFLECTION

Why is this issue so important for the people in the television industry?

The reality is that cable television inaugurated a new kind of television in America. Cable was largely unregulated and even uncensored. Thus the introduction of cable in the 1970s and 1980s was accompanied by a flood of programming that featured previously unimagined degrees of sex (including nudity), violence, and a kind of language that previously had been primarily reserved for back alleys and bar rooms.

When questioned about this content, many programming executives have answered with this standard response: "All we are doing is giving people more choice, and the ability to choose what they want."

> "WE DO NOT CHANGE VALUES OR ETHICS – WE JUST REFLECT THEM."

They have argued, "Cable programming is not responsible for the problems in the country," and "We do not change values or ethics – we just reflect them."

Yet to many people this has seemed to be a hollow argument. Many of us have argued that broadcasters are responsible for what they air. Amazingly, some seem to disagree with this.

HOW FAR WILL CABLE OPERATORS AND PROGRAMMERS GO IN "GIVING PEOPLE WHAT THEY WANT?"

The question has arisen, "Are there any limits to what programmers might provide?" Recent experience indicates that some do not see any limits. How far will cable operators and programmers go in "giving people what they want?" How much gambling, pornography, and the encouragement of drugs and immorality are they willing to "give" people?

Only a few voices have spoken out for the need to encourage religious beliefs, family values, and even common decency. "Our" task is to battle for these values within the industry, and make sure there is a place for the gospel in the media.

In fact one of our recent trade advertising campaigns has focused on proving to cable operators that religion is an important issue for millions of Americans. Many operators agree with us, but many others do not.

BY THEIR FRUITS

The "Voices Against Violence" campaign was in itself a

worthy cause. Yet, I was concerned that some of the efforts seemed to be hypocritical. Ironically, many of the leaders of this campaign were, in fact, representatives of organizations that were the most committed to violence, and the things they were apparently fighting.

This was demonstrated in 1997 with the release of a 3-year, $3.5 million National Television Violence study that was conducted by the National Cable Television Association (NCTA) by the University of California at Santa Barbara's Center for Communications and Social Policy. This revealed:

- Television programming continues to be *dominated by violence*, and the *amount of violent programming in primetime has steadily increased* during the past three years.
- Violent programming on the major broadcast networks has increased 14% in primetime since 1994, according to the study.
- Violent primetime programming on basic cable networks increased 10%.
- "Across the three years of the study, a steady *60% of TV programs contains violence*."
- Primetime programming with violence on network television increased from 53% to 67% during the last three years.
- Primetime violence on non-network stations increased from 70% to 77%.
- "The way most TV violence is portrayed continues to

pose risks to viewers."

- Much of TV violence is still glamorized. Good characters are frequently the perpetrators of violence, and rarely do they show remorse or experience negative repercussions for violence.
- Across the three years of this study, nearly *40% of the violent incidents on television are initiated by characters who possess qualities that make them attractive role models.*
- More than one third of violent programs feature "bad" characters who are never punished anywhere in the plot.
- Fully 71% of violent scenes contain no remorse, criticism, or penalty for violence at the time that it occurs.
- Roughly half of the violent incidents on television show no physical harm or pain to the victim.
- At least 40% of the violent scenes on television include humor.
- Less than 20% of the violent programs portray the long-term damage of violence to the victim's family, friends, and community.
- During prime-time, the percentage of programs that contain violence on the four broadcast networks has risen by 14% since 1994.

Yet, in spite of these findings from the industry's own research, little concrete action seems to be taking place . . . except for band-aid solutions like a ratings system.

CRYING "CENSORSHIP!"

I was asked to speak at a panel discussion on the topic of violence at a cable industry event. Another speaker was a representative of another cable network that had a history of focusing on violent programming. He adamantly defended their right to broadcast anything they wanted, and cried, "Censorship!" when it was suggested that they exercise more responsibility and restraint in their programming choices.

He seemed to ridicule me when I stated that cable networks had an obligation and social responsibility to hold up standards and police themselves. It was as though, speaking almost as the embodiment of the industry, he completely rejected any sense of responsibility to society.

Unfortunately, for every move forward, it seems there are two steps back. And the downward spiral continues.

In reality, we should not be too surprised. Christians should not be foolish enough to believe that the television industry itself is going to declare war on programming that attracts high ratings and has proven profitable! Let's not delude ourselves: The world will always choose money over morality.

> LET'S NOT DELUDE OURSELVES: THE WORLD WILL ALWAYS CHOOSE MONEY OVER MORALITY

SLEEPING WITH THE ENEMY

My father often used a phase in his sermons I have never forgotten: *All truth is parallel.*

In other words, this means that the principles that apply in one arena of life also apply in others.

If we were at war in America and enemy soldiers were trespassing on our soil, do you think we would be apathetic about such an invasion? Not on your life! We would secure our defenses and throw everything we have into the battle in order to defeat the intruders.

Our military forces are at their posts, always monitoring our borders, ready to send a warning should there be a hint of an invasion.

Today, an ungodly evil force has besieged our land. Yet who is on guard to detect the invasion? Where are the sentinels? How is the warning to be communicated?

> # WHO IS SOUNDING THE ALARM, AND WARNING THE PEOPLE?

As we look around today, it appears that many have abandoned their posts, and are no longer vigilantly on guard. Who is sounding the alarm, and warning the people?

Instead of putting on the whole armor of God and watching for sniper fire, many seem to be worried about their own affairs, and not concerned about the state of our world.

Even worse, many have invited the intruders inside and are sleeping with the enemy. The adversary has invaded our homes. He is here and many of us have capitulated, and even attempted to live in peace with him. We say, "If you don't bother me, I won't bother you."

If you are one of those people with this attitude, I have a message for you: Wake up! Don't abdicate your post!

The evidence is all around us. The enemy is everywhere, attacking, assaulting, and influencing God's people –

> # WAKE UP! DON'T ABDICATE YOUR POST!

through divorce, crime, sex, violence, and so much more.

WHERE IS THE WATCHMAN?

The people of God are supposed to be a "city set on a hill" (Matthew 5:14). God spoke to Ezekiel and said, "Son of man, speak to the children of your people, and say to them: 'When I bring the sword upon a land, and the people of the land take a man from their territory and make him their watchman . . . . But if the watchman sees the sword coming and does not blow the trumpet, and the people are not warned, and the sword comes and takes any person among them, he is taken away in his iniquity: but his blood I will require at the watchman's hand. So you, son of man: I have made you a watchman for the house of Israel; therefore you shall hear a word from My mouth and warn them for Me"

(Ezekiel 32:2, 6-7).

Many people have attempted to be the world's friend. We want the approval of the world, and are often afraid to tackle tough issues for fear of alienating someone. But we need to remember that Jesus said, "You will be hated by all for My name's sake" (Matthew 10:22).

Why do we find it so strange that we are despised by the world? Is this not what the Lord said would happen?

SENDING A MESSAGE

I recently attended a conference of Christian leaders in Colorado on the dangers of the Internet. After hours of discussion, one conclusion from those in the room was that government regulations are no match for a young person who wants to find perversion and pornography on the world wide web.

> THERE ARE A HANDFUL OF SHORT-TERM SOLUTIONS, YET NOTHING CAN COMPARE WITH A CHANGE OF HEART

There are a handful of short-term solutions, yet nothing can compare with a change of heart. That is why it is vital that we send a message of hope to the next generation, and provide quality alternatives for them that are based on Biblical values.

Do you think the headlines

of killings in schools are over? Sadly, this plague will continue. And it is not because mothers and fathers do not care. Most of them do.

For a moment, I want you to picture a mother coming home from the hospital with her newborn baby. What she is cradling in her arms is the object of love and pride.

Now, fast-forward the scene fifteen or twenty years later. What are you likely to see? In many cases, that sweet, innocent child has become a rebellious young adult who is involved in drugs, alcohol and sex.

What happened? What were the influences, or lack of influence, that brought about this radical change?

Most parents would agree that they should be the ones to shape their children's values, morals and ethics. But, let's face it, young people spend more time in front of the television set than in conversation or activities with their parents. The scales are weighed heavily in favor of the media's influence – and the darkness it brings.

> # THE SCALES ARE WEIGHED HEAVILY IN FAVOR OF THE MEDIA'S INFLUENCE

HUNGRY FOR REALITY

What was the response to the Columbine tragedy? Almost immediately there were psychological profiles being analyzed, counselors being consulted, and a host of government and media pundits offering their opinions. Yet most of these attempts did not address the root cause of the problem.

What is the root cause? What is the real answer?

We have taken God and prayer out of our schools, and that is exactly where parents, students, and school officials turned at the moment of crisis. Almost immediately we saw groups of students praying. At the funerals, there were invitations for people to accept Christ as their Savior. Should it not be clear that the only answer for the heart of man is the help, guidance, comfort, and salvation of the Lord?

> MOST OF OUR
> YOUNG PEOPLE
> ARE TENDER
> AND
> SPIRITUALLY
> HUNGRY

Our young people desperately need a Savior. Despite what at times looks like radical outward appearance, most of our young people are tender and spiritually hungry.

Day after day, commercial television sells them a pack of lies. We must counteract that message on every front – in the home, in the church, and through Christ-centered media.

Without a fixed position of true north, a compass is useless. And what would be the benefit of a weather vane that was constantly spinning in the wind?

Our society is in dire need of guidelines, parameters, and fixed laws to save itself from anarchy and mayhem. The principles found in God's Word are timeless. Unless they are adopted both inside and outside the church, our nation will continue to slide into a great abyss.

It is time to say, "Enough is enough." It is time to be on guard - man your post - be a watchman! And yes, get spiritually violent. Matt 11:12 says, "And from the days of John the Baptist until now the kingdom of heaven suffereth violence, and the violent take it by force." The choice is yours. You can capitulate to the enemy, or you can defend your territory, your family and loved ones against the onslaughts of the enemy. This is not a game. This is serious. Your spiritual destiny and that of your family is at stake.

CHAPTER SEVEN

THE POWER IS IN YOUR HANDS

C an one person make a difference? Absolutely.
In 1980, thirteen-year-old Cari Lightner was walking
along a city street when she was killed by a repeat-offender
drunk driver. Her mother, Candi, was appalled at the light
sentence given to the man who killed her daughter.

Candi Lightner – one determined individual – set out on
a campaign to bring about tougher laws against impaired
driving, stiffer penalties for committing such crimes, and a
greater awareness on the part of government and the public
concerning the seriousness of drunk driving.

Today, the organization she founded, Mother's Against
Drunk Driving (MADD) has over 600 chapters nationwide.

THE GUIDELINES

You may only be one individual, yet there is tremendous
power when you take a stand for something in which you
believe.

Where can you begin?

If you are the parents of young children, here are six important actions you need to take regarding the use of television:

1. **Make viewing time a family event.**
   Watch television with your children. Pay close attention to what they are viewing and discuss it with them.

2. **Set limits on time.**
   Only watch selected programs at specific pre-determined times.

3. **Discuss any act of violence.**
   If any offending scene, however small, appears on the screen, explain that in real life, violence causes pain and death. Let children know that these are only actors.

4. **Discuss any action or dialogue that condones immoral behavior or violates Biblical principles.**
   Many programs allow dialogue that is suggestive or encourages questionable behavior. This often is done with subtlety. Do not let these references go by. Be sensitive to them yourself, and point them out to your children.

5. **Turn off programs that contain violence and encourage immoral behavior.**
   Verbally disapprove of violence and immorality in front of your children. When it appears, turn off the television or change channels – and explain why. Let your children know that violence is not a way to resolve problems, and that no one should live by unbiblical principles.

6. Talk with other parents about the problem.
Seek a unified approach to handle the peer pressure.
As parents, however, set your own rules.

A SOLID FOUNDATION

My wife, Barbara, and I understood as parents of two children that it was our responsibility to nurture, instruct and instill in them Godly principles and values. We also believed it was our task to make certain God's Word and a personal relationship with Him was prominent in their lives.

Perhaps nothing was more important while our children were growing up than family devotions – a practice we still continue. It is a time of reading and studying the Word, praying and talking about the things of God.

The obligation to provide a strong foundation for our children included taking control over what they were exposed to and influenced by – especially television.

We need to know in advance, "What is the theme of this show?" "Does it contain a positive message?" The parent who does not have time to hand-pick what their children are viewing should remove the television set from the home. Such is the seriousness of the problem.

Christian parents have a responsibility to take charge

> CHRISTIAN PARENTS HAVE A RESPONSIBILITY TO TAKE CHARGE OF THE TELEVISION REMOTE CONTROL

of the television remote control. Make a vow to the Lord to be more vigilant concerning the messages the mass media is flooding into your home.

HUNGRY FOR TRUTH

What do I see when I look into the eyes of today's teens? Many seem to have lost their innocence at a very early age. They are hungry for reality, for truth – for identity and a sense of belonging.

Christian homes are not immune from the turmoil facing young people. I feel the pain of parents who have done the best they can, yet watch their children make wrong choices.

Barbara and I can relate to that. In some ways I am embarrassed to say it, but there was a time in both our children's lives when they were teenagers that we thought they had bought a one-way ticket to Hell, and there was no way back. Yet we could not give up on God, or our children. God is faithful. Today, our adult children, Ben and Becky, are both serving the Lord.

The greatest desire and prayer Christian parents should have for their teens is to see them surrender to the Lordship of Jesus Christ.

CHANGING BOUNDARIES

When children become teenagers, the concern of the parents broadens from the input they are receiving from television to the messages they hear from music and through music videos.

We are not with our children twenty-four hours a day and media is difficult to monitor. As one parent told me, "It is difficult to teach our teens what they *should not* listen to, when we frankly do not know what they *are* listening to."

The average teen listens to music forty hours a week – often with headsets of their portable CD's blocking out sounds of the real world. And, when they do switch to television viewing, it is likely to watch music videos of what they have been listening to.

Psychologists examining such behavior say, "It is part of their identity." However, you cannot listen to forty hours of rock music lyrics every week without absorbing the message. Over time, the social boundaries we have worked so hard to establish have been redefined. Their perception of "okay" behavior has been radically changed.

In the absence of a sound family structure – where parents and kids can converse openly about issues – there is a vacuum. It is often filled by music that is ultimately socially and morally damaging.

To get a real-world education, sample a few "rap," "punk rock" and "hard rock" songs on the radio. They are frequently peppered with obscenity, profanity, vulgarity and blasphemy – counterfeit messages Satan is trying to perpetrate on our youth.

> IT IS SYMPTOMATIC OF A PROBLEM THAT LIES MUCH DEEPER IN OUR CULTURE

I believe what is being communicated is not only destructive, but has an evil root. The message instills a dangerous and dark influence in the lives of young people – and it is symptomatic of a problem that lies much deeper in our culture.

The effect of music on teen behavior is no longer a debate. Teenagers idolize pop stars and emulate their fashion, talk and mannerisms. Even more, they act out messages found in the music.

WHAT IS THE MESSAGE?

In fairness, some of the secular music of the past decades, and still today, have included lyrics that are positive and uplifting. There have been memorable love songs, and music that was fun and entertaining.

Most of what young people are being exposed to now, however, are lyrics from a sub-culture that increasingly presents a shocking, negative message. They glorify violence, encourage standards and behavior that often violate Biblical principles, and preach hatred, abuse and permissiveness.

If parents took the time to listen to the lyrics, they would be appalled.

> IF PARENTS TOOK THE TIME TO LISTEN TO THE LYRICS, THEY WOULD BE APPALLED

Music sets a mood or a tone and communicates with great emotion. It has a language of its own and can be either good or bad. The determining factor is the *message* contained in the words.

DEATH OR LIFE?

According to Scripture the words we hear and speak are spirit and life. The Bible declares that "Death and life are in the power of the tongue" (Proverbs 18:21). And Jesus said, "For by your words you will be justified, and by your words you will be condemned" (Matthew 12:37).

God is not against music. It is one of His great creations. We are told to "Break forth in song, rejoice, and sing praises. Sing to the Lord . . . With the harp and the sound of a psalm, With trumpets and the sound of a horn; Shout joyfully before the Lord, the King" (Psalms 98:4-6).

The angels sang to herald the birth of Jesus – and there is coming a day when a trumpet from heaven will signal the great rapture of the church.

No, music by itself is not good or bad. It is the message of the music that speaks either life or death.

We must control the message that we are allowing to be taken into our spirits – and to the extent possible, the spirits of our children. Those seeds are going to bring forth a good or evil harvest.

> IT IS THE MESSAGE OF THE MUSIC THAT SPEAKS EITHER LIFE OR DEATH

SCREENING AND FILTERING

The average parent does not have a clue what their children are listening to. In their attempt to respect privacy, they allow their teens a free hand to choose whatever music they wish. There is no screening – no filtering.

If you hand your child $12 or $15 to buy a new CD, do you not also have the right to listen to the music they are buying?

Here is how one dad kept his son's music on track. When the son brought a new album into the home, they sat down and listened together – even though it was not the style of music the father enjoyed.

> ## "I'D BETTER BE CAREFUL ABOUT THE MUSIC I BRING HOME."

The son quickly came to the conclusion, "I'd better be careful about the music I bring home."

Parents can also help provide an alternative. Some of the most highly acclaimed rock music today is being produced by contemporary Christian artists. There are now *millions* who are fans of this "positive" rock.

At INSP we have created a block of time in our schedule called "Music Zone." It is youth-oriented programming that is both relevant and uplifting.

FOUR KEYS

There are four keys every parent needs to use to help reach this generation of teens.

1. **Involvement.**
   Get involved with your teenagers. Be a part of their life as much as possible.
2. **Prayer.**
   Never, ever stop praying for them – or *with* them.
3. **Belief.**
   From our heart we need to express confidence in their future. We must never give up on them.
4. **Love.**
   Our love must be unconditional. They may commit

acts we disapprove of, yet we must never allow that disapproval to become rejection.

IT IS IN YOUR HAND

Before the children of Israel began their journey through the wilderness, God called Moses and asked, "What is in your hand?" (Exodus 4:2).

He answered, "I've got this staff."

The Lord said, "Throw it down on the ground and see what I can make out of it."

God took something that was ordinary in the hand of Moses and turned it into something supernatural.

I have heard people say, "If I were wealthy and powerful, here is what I would do."

The Lord is not asking "What if?" He wants to know, "What is in your hand?" In other words, what will you do with what you have? That is where the miracles begin.

> ## HE WANTS TO KNOW, "WHAT IS IN YOUR HAND?"

I remember hearing a song with the words: "Little becomes much when you put it in the Master's hands!"

Your act of changing the world may be as simple as pressing the "off" button on the remote control when offensive material appears on a program. Or, you may take a pen and piece of paper and write a letter to the sponsor of a show you find offensive.

My duty is exactly like yours. God has placed something in my hand – in my case it is a cable television network. I must do whatever I can to see evangelism and discipleship go forward.

Your Covenant

Today, I am asking you to make a covenant with God regarding what you will watch, listen to or speak from this day forward. Say to the Lord:

MAKE A COVENANT WITH GOD REGARDING WHAT YOU WILL WATCH, LISTEN TO OR SPEAK

- I make a covenant that my eyes will not look upon those things that are not pleasing in Your sight.
- I make a covenant that my ears will not listen to music or language that is vulgar or profane.
- I make a covenant that my lips will not speak words that would harm or injure.
- I make a covenant to encourage my family to watch, listen to, and experience only that which upholds my Christian faith and Biblical principles.

The psalmist wrote, "I will behave wisely in a perfect way. Oh, when will You come to me? I will walk within my house with a perfect heart. I will set nothing wicked before my eyes; I hate the work of those who fall away; It shall not cling to me. A perverse heart shall depart from me; I will not know

104

wickedness" (Psalms 101:2-4).

Let me ask that you find a place alone with God and spend time in prayer regarding each of these covenants. Make a commitment that you will not only be the guardian of what enters your eyes and ears, but you will be an example to those who are looking to you for guidance.

Remember, *the power is in your hands!*

CHAPTER EIGHT

KEEPERS OF THE AQUARIUM?

W hat is our responsibility as Christians to use the media to influence this generation? How do some in "religious" broadcasting define the role of Christian television today? How do we use the media to reach the masses?

I once had the opportunity to ask a number of friends, who are also Christian leaders, to define the mission of Christian television.

Dr. Richard Lee, pastor of First Redeemer Church in Alpharetta, Georgia, and host of *There's Hope,* replied that "Christian television is programming that fulfills the great commission of our Lord . . . The purpose our Lord gave in Matthew, Chapter 28 was, 'to win, to baptize, teach and disciple every person possible until Jesus comes again. Christian television is to represent Christ in our society, His love and compassion and, of course, His message of hope for the hopeless.'"

Dr. John Hagee, pastor of Cornerstone Church in San Antonio, Texas, and host of *John Hagee Today* stated, "The mission and the role of Christian television in society today is the fulfilling of the Great Commission. Christian television is television that advances Bible principles of the Judeo-Christian faith . . . and enforces the absolute reliance upon the Word of God as direction for our lives."

Well-known pastor Dr. Charles Stanley, pastor of First Baptist Church in Atlanta, Georgia, and host of the television program *In Touch*, sees the mission "to make a very clear presentation of the gospel. I see our role as impacting society, right where we are now in business, in school, in every area of our society."

My dad, world renowned author and evangelist, and host of the television program *Victory with Morris Cerullo*, said, "The purpose of Christian television is to do more than just speak to the choir and when I say that, I mean those that are in the Church. Christian television has an incredible responsibility to be able to reach out to those that are beyond the four walls of the Church and touch them with the message of our Lord and Savior, Jesus Christ."

Let me take the liberty of summarizing what I believe these men of God, and so many others I have talked to on this important subject, are saying. It is simply this: the mission of Christian television is two-fold – Evangelism and Discipleship.

The role of Christian television is constant and timeless.

However, I believe what our mission is *supposed to be*, and what it actually *is* (or has become) are two entirely different things.

NEW DELIVERY SYSTEMS

In the Sermon on the Mount in Matthew, Chapter 5, Jesus told us that we are "the light of the world." The function of the Body of Christ is much like a lighthouse – providing a beacon that shows people the way to go. To illuminate dangerous and treacherous cliffs and rocks, those things to avoid and to help people find their way to a new life in Christ.

> THE FUNCTION OF THE BODY OF CHRIST IS MUCH LIKE A LIGHTHOUSE

Here we are, two thousand years later. The message is still the same. Jesus is the light of the world. However, the structure of the "lighthouse"– the medium, the delivery systems for the message has been changing, and the power of the medium has multiplied many times over.

For centuries Christians have been using every means possible to communicate the Gospel and fulfill the Great Commission. First starting by word of mouth only. As times and technologies evolved, more tools have been placed at our disposal to communicate and share the gospel. As a result of these advances, the message is being preached on a scale as never before.

The introduction of the printing press, global transportation, mass communication, radio, television, satellite, high speed data transmission, computers and the Internet are just a few examples. Faster and more economical computer chips are swinging open even more doors.

As the Body of Christ, we must recognize the revolution that is taking place in both the structure and the power of these mediums – and we must respond! This is not a time for business as usual.

THE ROLE OF THE CHURCH

When the Apostle Paul described the ministry or role of the Church in Ephesians he said, "And he gave some, apostles; and some, prophets; and some, evangelists; and some, pastors and teachers; For the perfecting of the saints, for the work of the ministry, for the edifying of the body of Christ: Till we all come in the unity of the faith, and of the knowledge of the Son of God, unto a perfect man, unto the measure of the stature of the fullness of Christ" (Ephesians 4:11-13).

It seems to me that four out of the five functions or purposes of the Church deal with focusing their attention inwards towards the body of Christ – the apostle, the prophet, the pastor, the teacher. The office of the evangelist is the only office targeted to going out and "fishing for men."

Perhaps that is why so much Christian television today seems to be aimed inwards towards the Body of Christ.

Maybe it is the reason so many observers have suggested that we are "preaching to the choir." I believe most Christian television has become a "keeper of the aquarium" rather than a "fisher of men."

Yes, the Body of Christ needs "keeping." It needs *strengthening, encouraging* and *perfecting* – as the Apostle Paul wrote. It longs for someone to equip it through the ministry of the Word. All of that is needed, and we want to facilitate that as much as possible. That is why one of

> I BELIEVE MOST CHRISTIAN TELEVISION HAS BECOME A "KEEPER OF THE AQUARIUM" RATHER THAN A "FISHER OF MEN."

our roles must be to initiate and support programming which attempts to "perfect the saints for the work of the ministry."

Equally, however, we must turn our attention outward. There is a world "out there" that many of our "traditional religious programs" are not reaching that needs to hear the Good News of the gospel. In fact, over three billion people living today have never yet one time heard the gospel!

We cannot abandon the world to the secular, humanistic, and dark influences that daily flood the television airwaves. We must reach out to those who either have not heard the message, or have not made Jesus Christ the Lord of their life.

Many viewers are turned off by *their* perception of what religious television is. Most of the so-called secular world has become so familiar with traditional religious programs that they can identify them within a fraction of a second, and their finger, which is already poised on the remote control, is changing to another channel. Is it any wonder? Scripture so clearly tells us that "the natural man does not receive the things of the Spirit of God, for they are foolishness to him; nor can he know them, because they are spiritually discerned" (1 Corinthians 2:14).

COMPELLING METHODS

If we are ever going to use movies, television, the Internet, video games or other media to effectively reach the lost we are going to have to first produce *content* and *programming* that will capture people's imagination and cause them to watch.

THE NUMBER ONE REASON PEOPLE TURN ON TELEVISION . . . IS TO BE ENTERTAINED

Let's face it, the number one reason people turn on television, go to the movies or play a video game is to be entertained. Therefore, if we are going to "pull in the net" we have got to find compelling methods of communicating the gospel. We must discover ways to "package" the message – for our generation and those who will follow – in a way that will compel them to watch, and in a "language" they understand.

Following the example given by the Apostle Paul, so much of today's "religious programming" has become targeted to Christians:
- It is *by* Christians.
- It is *for* Christians.
- It is *about* Christianity.

The "lost," as God's Word would define them, are simply not watching Christ-centered television in large numbers.

Don't misunderstand me. I realize that many people do come to know Jesus Christ as their Lord and Savior by watching traditional Christian programs. And, I praise God for that! But sadly, the reality is that statistically, the number of people who come to Christ in this manner is a very small percentage of those influenced by non-Christian television.

One of my dreams is to see a future where traditional religious-Christian programming can be supplemented (not eliminated) and complemented with broad-based, wholesome, life-enriching, engaging, entertaining, inspirational and redemptive programming which supports the Christian world view and the values we as believers cherish and embrace – programming that reaches outside the aquarium!

REACHING OUTSIDE THE AQUARIUM

As believers we need to utilize the medium of television to influence the values, beliefs and behavior of people for Christ. The most important thing we can influence is their relationship to God, then to their family and their fellow man.

In that regard, Christian television should develop programming which penetrates outside the four walls of the church, physically and electronically, and targets its message towards those who have not made Jesus Christ the Lord of their life. Most importantly, it needs to have a message which directs people to a personal relationship with the Savior.

Unfortunately, most Christ-centered television has lost sight of this second objective. Almost none of our so-called "Christian" programming is reaching very far outside the church (or the body of Christ) to a lost world.

JESUS' METHOD

One of Jesus' most effective preaching techniques was His use of parables – He told stories with a message that touched people because of their relationship to real life. The parables cut across geopolitical, social, racial, historic and other barriers. By this example, Jesus demonstrated that His followers could reach the world by using stories.

> WE CAN *SHOW* PEOPLE HOW TO LIVE INSTEAD OF ONLY *TELLING* THEM

Via television we can do the same. We can *show* people how to live instead of only *telling* them. Our challenge is to find innovative ways to communicate a message of hope, redemption, salvation, peace, healing and restoration in a variety of formats – children's programs, news, sports, game shows, sitcoms and drama. However, before we can communicate a message, we must first attract people to watch.

DUAL CITIZENSHIP

The world walks in a different direction, has different desires, and speaks a different language. Unfortunately, secular society is characterized in

> BEFORE WE CAN COMMUNICATE A MESSAGE, WE MUST FIRST ATTRACT PEOPLE TO WATCH

large part by the pleasure-values of this world. These are the people described in the Bible "whose end is destruction, whose god is their belly, and whose glory is in their shame; who set their mind on earthly things" (Philippians 3:19).

The world longs for more wealth, power, and personal aggrandizement. They believe that "since you go around only once, grab for all the gusto you can." Their values are based on human desire. It seems that tolerance for every form of deviance has become a national icon to them.

Christians are supposed to have different aspirations. We are to know the difference between the temporary and the permanent. We are to arrive at different destinations. What is the end of this world? Destruction. Unbelievers are alienated from God both in *this life* and in the world to come.

As Christians we are supposed to be "in the world," but

not "of the world" (John 17:13-14). And we must become "salt and light" with such spiritual power that society will be transformed.

HOPING FOR ACCOLADES?

Why are we so uptight about the media declaring war on our Christian values? What do we *expect* from people who don't know Christ? Are we hoping for accolades? Why should we think that the gospel would be attractive to the world when the Bible pointedly says that it contains a message that will be greeted with hostility? Jesus declared, "If the world hates you, you know that it hated Me before it hated you" (John 15:18).

Why should we expect Hollywood to reflect Christian values when our culture as a whole does not?

So what do we do?

I believe we must return to those truths that made the church great. We must put on the whole armor of God. And we must go out into the world and do spiritual battle. We must proclaim a message that is nothing less than the direct intervention of God in society. We must be like Christ, who never wavered from His message of spiritual redemption.

> WE MUST RETURN TO THOSE TRUTHS THAT MADE THE CHURCH GREAT

116

The Bible alone is God's Word. It reveals the Father's character and nature to us – His grace, His mercy, His forgiveness, His love. The Bible is our guidebook, our manual, our standard for living. It shows us how to live an overcoming life, how to wage spiritual warfare and how to have victory over the enemy. It sets forth God's standards and expectations. Jesus said that He was "the way, the truth and the life." He did not say that he was *a* way, or *a* truth, or *a* life. This means that all other religions – all prophets, gurus, and revelations must line up with the Word of God or be rejected.

It is a message that must be heard again in our day of pluralism and pop religion.

Salvation cannot be the work of man, but must be the work of God alone.

We must keep pointing beyond this life to the next and encourage others to join us on our pilgrimage.

A THREE-CHANNEL WORLD

Consider the changes that have occurred in the era of television and specifically *Christian* television. Forty years ago, things were much more simple, and frankly, quite limited. In those days we lived in a three-channel world of ABC, NBC and CBS.

There were only a few Christian programs to watch, and the primary focus was on evangelism and outreach. As times and technology improved, more and more choices became available which added to the complexity. Today, the average cable television system offers over 50 different channels. The direct broadcasting satellite companies who distribute programming to our homes via the small satellite dishes offer over 150 channels. And broadcast television is being challenged by new delivery methods such as cable, DBS, and the Internet.

Today there are over 125 ministries who produce and distribute Christian programs – most of which are aimed toward strengthening and equipping the body of Christ rather than evangelism.

It is time for those in Christian media to re-think how we deliver the message of hope to a hurting world.

LIFE-AFFIRMING STORIES

Let me pose the question to you. If people are watching to be entertained . . . if the natural man does not receive the things of God . . . if our traditional religious programs are not attracting much viewership from the world, (which, by the way, is what every Nielsen rating has ever said) . . . then what makes us think we can reach the secular audience with traditional religious programming?

According to so many of the trend-watchers today such as Barna, Gallup, CNN, US News & World Report and others, millions of people profess a belief in God, a Christian faith, and basic Biblical values. On the other hand, we see that most of the highest rated programs on television lack any morality base whatsoever. Unfortunately, market research informs us that Christians watch these programs long before they will tune into a traditional religious program.

The essence of our mission to impact the world is to produce, air and promote programs that show people how to live successfully throughout this journey called life. Yet we must respect the viewer's ability to make ultimate selections and decisions themselves – and demonstrate values or underlying themes by example and content instead of labeling.

The life-affirming stories presented must be based on real people and genuine experiences. And all of this needs to point to the *giver* of life, Jesus Christ.

TAPPING THE RESOURCES

America was built on the foundation of hard work, strong families, honesty, civic responsibility, obeying the law and respect for authority. What is the origin of these values? The Bible!

I believe passionately in the need for Christian television. Sadly, we have allowed the world to squeeze us into its own mold and put us in a box it has designed. And some of the blame rests on our shoulders. We have limited our impact and narrowly defined what

> WE HAVE ALLOWED THE WORLD TO SQUEEZE US INTO ITS OWN MOLD AND PUT US IN A BOX IT HAS DESIGNED

kinds of programs we can produce.

The challenge before us is *to use all the resources God has given us.* Jesus said, "I send you out as sheep in the midst of wolves. Therefore be wise as serpents and harmless as doves" (Matthew 10:16).

> ## "I SEND YOU OUT AS SHEEP IN THE MIDST OF WOLVES."
> *– MATTHEW 10:16*

One of my favorite pictures of Jesus is in His role as a fisher of men. Throughout His ministry, He spoke in terms people understood, and went to the places they lived and worked. He reached out to tax collectors, Samaritans, centurions, and individuals throughout society.

TIMELESS TRUTHS

As a Christian broadcaster I have a responsibility not merely to produce programs with which we are comfortable. We need to reach people where they are – in their homes – and communicate the timeless truth of the Gospel in formats they will watch. There are untold millions we are not reaching, who are not part of our culture, and who do not relate to what we have traditionally offered.

In recent months we have talked with Christian and non-Christian consumers, met with producers, writers, agencies, corporate heads and Christian business leaders. What we have discovered is that there are literally thousands of influential people who share our burden.

It is time the Body of Christ united – to put aside differences, fund fresh programming ventures, develop new enterprises and find maximum methods to impact the world with the gospel.

I believe this is one way we can fulfill the Great Commission in our lifetime. We must be fishers of men.

CHAPTER NINE

DOES ANYBODY CARE?

A young girl was walking along the seashore when she noticed hundreds of star fish that had washed up along the beach with the incoming tide.

She quickly stopped to pick them up, as she was walking along, knowing that if they did not make it back into the sea they would dry out in the hot sun and die. One by one, she tossed the star fish back into the ocean.

"What are you doing?" inquired a fisherman who was shore fishing near by.

"I'm saving the star fish," replied the young girl. "If they do not make it back into the water, they will die."

The fisherman, shaking his head, looked at the girl and said, "You cannot possibly save all these star fish, there are so many you can't even count them!" And he asked, "What difference does it make?"

The young lady, looking down at the sand, picked up

another one and tossed it into the ocean. "It made a difference to *that* one!" she exclaimed.

THE MISSION

The mission of INSP is very simple – to change the world for good, one life at a time, through television. It is much like rescuing star fish! We pray that God will use this to make a positive difference in the values, beliefs and behavior of people. Most importantly, it is people's relationship to God that we want to try and help "get right." Like the story of the pastor and his son that I shared with you in an earlier chapter, we believe that if we can get the "man right," we can get the "world right." So, one program at a time, one life at a time we are pursuing the dreams, visions and destiny that God has given us.

We wrestle with some important issues:

- How can television be used to fulfill the Great Commission?
- How can we utilize the media to share the *Good News* of God's love more effectively?
- What are the creative program formats that will in fact, influence the values, beliefs and behavior of people for Christ?
- What is the best way for us to be effective keepers of the aquarium *and* fishers of men?
- How do we pay for the cost of producing all this programming?

We want to provide Christians with a network they can turn to – not only in time of trouble, but also for their "daily bread" – a network which presents the best in teaching and preaching programs. And, a network that also presents Christ-centered entertaining programming for their young children, their teens and their entire family – programming that shows us how to live; that is life-enriching, engaging, informative, motivational, entertaining, inspiring and redemptive.

WHY WE INVEST

To reach the lost, the world, we must make the gospel presentation *unavoidable.* Our programming must be of the highest quality. We are not going to reach the lost by producing programs that do not equal or surpass the quality the world is delivering.

> WE MUST MAKE THE GOSPEL PRESENTATION *UNAVOIDABLE*

In recent years, INSP has produced dozens of original television series and specials. Let me give you an example.

We have dedicated a special time period Monday through Friday for young children. It is called "INSP for Kidz," and is hosted by a "live-action" character named Discovery Jones.

Discovery Jones is designed to be a Godly, male role model and appeal to kids ages 4 to 8.

According to government statistics, almost 17 million children live in homes with a mother and no father – and, let me remind you, nearly five million children spend time as what some refer to as "latchkey kids" – children without any adult supervision after school because mom and dad are working.

In addition to Discovery Jones, we have managed to produce or acquire other quality children's programs including Tom Sawyer, Jungle Book, Little Women, Swiss Family Robinson and the Donut Repair Club.

We feel it is important to sow into the lives of our children. They need programs that tell of God's unconditional love, how He sent His Son Jesus to die for them, and that their sins can be forgiven. So many children today live without the benefit of a "dad" at home. Unfortunately many others have an ungodly father as an example. If our children have a difficult time relating to an earthly father, how will they ever relate to a Heavenly Father?

Market research statistics from a number of evangelical organizations indicate that most people come to know Jesus Christ as their personal Lord and Savior before the age of 14! Think of it. That underscores the importance of impacting young minds and hearts with principals that will lead them to live responsible, moral, successful lives resembling a Godly lifestyle and value system as adults.

Our children's programming, like all of our original programming is not revenue producing. It is all an expense – all outgo and no income or revenue. Yet we feel a solemn obligation before God to reach this generation of young children with the gospel. That is why we have made a significant investment in the lives of our children with this type of programming.

These are returns no stock market investment can ever match!

One thing is for certain, the so-called secular or commercial television networks are not going to produce this kind of life-changing television programming. They do not offer much in the way of a positive, moral product for children, let alone something that is Godly or Christ-centered.

> # THESE ARE RETURNS NO STOCK MARKET INVESTMENT CAN EVER MATCH!

MAKING AN IMPACT

In addition to our focus on children, The Inspirational Network has created and produced many outstanding programs featuring investigative reports, Biblically-based stories, southern gospel music, programs for teens, clean comedy shows, contemporary Christian music videos, issue-oriented programs, Christian movies, and others.

Plus, INSP has long been recognized as a quality leader in the production of major Christian television specials and events – such as *Night of Joy* from Walt Disney World; *Jubilaté,* a New Year's Eve celebration featuring Bill and Gloria Gaither; the *True Love Waits National Celebration* from Washington DC; the *Hearts Aflame Awards; The Mark & Kathy Show* hosted by Mark Lowry and Kathy Troccoli; *Cheyenne Country Live* with John Schneider; *INSP's Family Cinema, The Inspirational Awards,* to name a few.

Each one of the television specials was both entertaining and evangelistic in its presentation. Take just one program as an example, the *True Love Waits* event and television special. In this one event we were a part of seeing over forty thousand teens pledge to keep themselves sexually pure before marriage.

We are grateful for what has been accomplished, yet recognize there is much more that needs to be done!

GUILT-FREE TV

The financial investment INSP has made to produce these series and specials has been significant – though we cannot compare our costs with those of the major networks. NBC, CBS or ABC easily spend over a million dollars per episode for most programs in prime-time viewing. At times we feel overwhelmed, as David surely felt when he faced Goliath. Yet we know God is on our side.

Because of the dedicated, talented staff of writers, producers and directors we have assembled, we are able to create first-rate programming for a fraction of what it costs in New York or Los Angeles.

Our objectives are to produce:

■ Comedy that makes you laugh without mocking

your beliefs.
- Movies and drama that reflect Biblical values.
- Children and teen programs that edify as well as entertain.
- Blockbuster specials throughout the year.
- Ministry programs that enlighten and encourage you in your faith.

Like most Americans, as a child you probably learned virtuous values such as sharing, honesty, respect and character – and as an adult you continue to believe in them. You wish you could turn on the TV without being turned off by foul language, vulgar jokes, violence and immoral behavior. And you wish you could watch TV with your entire family without embarrassment. That is the kind of programming we are committed to.

The networks will continue to produce shows flaunting relationships that run counter to Biblical traditional family values – content that exploits sexual humor, innuendo and gratuitous violence.

> YOU WISH YOU COULD TURN ON THE TV WITHOUT BEING TURNED OFF BY FOUL LANGUAGE, VULGAR JOKES, VIOLENCE AND IMMORAL BEHAVIOR

129

How does a network like INSP compete with that? We do not. And we will not even try. Our objective is not to skirmish with the darkness and be overcome ourselves, but to let the light of Jesus Christ shine through us, through our programming to illuminate the world and overcome the darkness.

I agree with the words of St. Francis of Assisi, "Start by doing what is necessary, then what is possible, and suddenly you are doing the impossible."

JUST ONE LIFE

We received an e-mail from an eight year old girl who said "Discovery Jones" explained how Jesus loved her and that if she would accept Him into her heart her life would be different. She wrote, "I just want to know if I do that, will my daddy stop beating me?"

> "WILL MY DADDY STOP BEATING ME?"

Where does that child turn to find something – *anything* – that is going to feed her soul, give her hope – and let her know that somebody cares?

A woman in New York City sent a letter saying that, after working late, she returned to her home "lonely, depressed and despondent." She turned on her television set and tuned to INSP. At that moment we were running one of our praise and worship programs entitled *Celebration*. She wrote: "It lifted my soul – I could sense the very presence of God and

I am so glad you were there for me."

Once, while taping a music special we assembled a small orchestra and one of the musicians apparently was not a Christian. During the rehearsal, the presence of the Lord was unmistakable in the praise and worship music. It was powerful!

When the session concluded, the musician came to us and said, "I've never felt anything like this! What is this?" And because of that experience we were able to lead him to Christ.

In our *Night of Joy* program from Disney World we saw literally thousands of people give their hearts to Christ in one single night, in one single program.

I could give you many examples of lives changed for eternity. This is what it is all about!

A NEW ERA

God has promised that in the last days, "I will pour out My Spirit on all flesh; Your sons and your daughters shall prophesy, Your old men shall dream dreams, Your young men shall see visions" (Joel 2:28).

We believe that prophecy is being fulfilled today in part through INSP and the vision God has given us.

Today, we are witnessing the dawn of a new era in communication that will eclipse all the technological advances that previously have shaped society. Simply put, *everything* as we have known it in television, radio, and the media is *about to change!*

With such sweeping transformations on the immediate horizon, the temptation is to react with fear or uncertainty. But we believe that this will be a time of unparalleled opportunity for Christians in broadcasting. New resources will open doors never before imagined for the gospel.

However, the awe-inspiring changes before us will not alter the basic needs of the human heart.

Indeed, this will force us in Christian media to re-evaluate what we do and how we do it. We have been seeking God's guidance as we travel this new avenue – dedicated to secure a strong place for the gospel in the superhighway of the future. We believe it will create expanded opportunities to reach people.

Paul wrote, "A great and effective door has opened to me, and there are many adversaries" (1 Corinthians 16:9).

The needs have never been greater. The opposition has never been more intense. But, the opportunities have never been more abundant.

> INSTEAD OF WAITING IN THE NIGHT, WE HAVE DECIDED TO TAKE A STAND

You may say, "I have 70 channels of programming coming into my home. What possible difference can one channel make?"

When you walk into a dark room and ignite the smallest flame it is amazing how much darkness it dispels.

Instead of waiting in the night, we have decided to take a

stand, to make a start, to put to use whatever God places into our hands, to make a difference.

Doors are opening for us. Books are available to be turned into screenplays for movies and programs. We have received proposals from award-winning writers, producers, and actors. Recording artists and record companies want to develop more concerts and alternative inspirational entertainment. High quality concepts for children, teens, and adults are ready to go into production. We have a state-of-the-art production facility under the direction of some of the finest editors, producers, and engineers in the country.

Yet all of this takes commitment, and resources. We need people to stand with us to make this dream a reality, and light a candle that will dispel darkness!

Does anybody care? We do. And I believe you do also!

CHAPTER TEN

HOW YOU CAN CHANGE YOUR WORLD FOR GOOD

There are two ways to fight. One, in the spirit – the other, in the natural.

What is the cure for darkness? In the natural, the answer is not isolationism, but confrontation. We need to confront the darkness with the right attitude and the right message. Yet all of our efforts will be useless unless we go to the root of the problem – which lies in the spirit realm. We must declare war *spiritually,* and take the *spiritual* offensive. We must confront the world with the one message that is able to truly change the world – one life at a time.

Every day Satan and his demons are trying to influence people for evil. The battle we spoke of earlier still rages and people must decide whether they will listen to God or Satan.

In Scripture, God calls His angels "ministering spirits." In a way, Satan's angels can also be considered ministering spirits. One ministers life, the other death.

I remember President Reagan calling communist Russia "the evil empire." Today we need to ask, "What – or who – is the *real* enemy?" Our focus in this volume has been on television, which is an inanimate object, neither good nor evil. It is simply a tool; a piece of technology. Our rallying cry cannot be against TV, or the people who provide it. Rather, we must confront the forces and influences which have produced this condition.

> ## TODAY WE NEED TO ASK, "WHAT – OR WHO – IS THE *REAL* ENEMY?"

For too long we have allowed the devil to use television as a means to accomplish his agenda. He brings satanic negative influences against the minds of people who control the content of television – and those influences are brought against the everyday person.

GOOD OR EVIL?

I remember being in Brazil years ago for what was called "The Million Soul Crusade" with my father and his ministry, Morris Cerullo World Evangelism. The objective of this particular event was two-fold, evangelism and discipleship. For one entire week, Monday through Friday, over 15,000 national Brazilian pastors gathered together, via satellite-delivered television, in nine different convention centers and cities across Brazil. They came to be strengthened and better equipped to do the work of ministry. They came to learn how they could "work the works of God" (John 6:28).

Then, on Saturday night the emphasis of the event changed to evangelism as we moved from the convention centers in these nine cities to large stadiums for a crusade service. The crusade was also transmitted via satellite to over 100 different cities across the United States, Canada and the Far East. One objective of The Million Soul Crusade was for my dad to be able to present the gospel to a million people, in one single night. It was a revolutionary concept. At that time it had only been done once by the Billy Graham organization, yet not on this scale.

TELEVISION IS A TOOL

The pastors in Brazil, especially the Pentecostal clergy, were outspoken adversaries of television. Some went as far as to say, "If you have a television set in your home, you are not welcome to fellowship at our church." In effect, people were being excommunicated.

I was having a difficult time breaking through the barriers that these leaders had erected against television.

> "IF YOU HAVE A TELEVISION SET IN YOUR HOME, YOU ARE NOT WELCOME TO FELLOWSHIP AT OUR CHURCH."

Because our meetings were being delivered via satellite and television-type screens (large screen image magnification systems), they were refusing to encourage their pastors and congregations to participate in the meetings.

I immediately scheduled a private leadership conference and invited all the various denominational leaders from across Brazil. The attendance was fantastic! Almost every major denominational leader in that nation came. I asked, "How many have brought your Bibles to the meeting?" Almost every hand shot up.

> ## "HOW MANY HAVE BROUGHT YOUR BIBLES TO THE MEETING?"

Then I questioned the ministers if they knew where their Bibles were printed? No one did. I asked if they would be surprised to know that most likely the same presses that printed their Bibles were also used to produce pornography – one of the leading categories of printed matter in Brazil.

The point I was making was quickly understood. The printing press was a tool – it was not good or evil by itself. Yet what it produced was either uplifting or degrading, depending on what people decided to print. The pastors in Brazil quickly shifted their support completely behind the meetings. As a result, we saw thousands of national Brazilian pastors trained, and yes, in one night, tens of thousands of people across Brazil, the United States, Canada and the Far East gave their hearts to the Lord Jesus Christ!

What was true of the printing press was equally true of television – it is merely a delivery system. The enemy we must effectively target is not television, but Satan.

A NEW KINGDOM

We bemoan our current circumstances, yet at the time of Christ's birth, there was great uncertainty and turmoil – particularly for the people who tried to serve God. The

> THE ENEMY WE MUST EFFECTIVELY TARGET IS NOT TELEVISION, BUT SATAN

days when Israel was a sovereign nation seemed like fiction of a far distant past. The accounts of great victories in battle, the fear that Israel struck in the hearts of many people, and the miracles that demonstrated God's willingness to show Himself strong on behalf of His chosen people Israel, were like fables.

The Jews of that era, like millions of others, were dominated by the greatest power the world had known until that moment: the Roman empire.

Its control over the life of the Jews seemed complete. What freedoms they enjoyed were theirs only because of the will of the Romans.

Moreover, the Jews had a record of recent failure to draw upon. Efforts to overthrow Roman rule had been ruthlessly crushed. The people and ruling political, civil, and religious authorities, seemed to have decided that acceptance of their subservient state and submission to Rome was their only hope.

Later, as Pilate was deciding Jesus' sentence, the chief priests confirmed the state of their existence: "We have no king but Caesar" (John 19:15).

The angel announcing Jesus' birth to Mary said that "he will rule over the house of Jacob forever; his kingdom will never end" (Luke 1:33). Indeed, the prophet Isaiah had written this prophecy more than five hundred years earlier: "Of the increase of his government and peace there will be no end" (Isaiah 9:7).

How hollow these words could have sounded! How hopeless many of the people could have felt!

> ## HE INTRODUCED A KINGDOM THAT COULD NOT BE SHAKEN

Yet Jesus *did* come to the earth. He *did* live and bring the kingdom of God to people in a way they could never have imagined. He did not bring them military or political victory over Rome. Instead He introduced a kingdom that could not be shaken, a faith that sees the reality of spiritual truth and anointing, and a power from the Holy Spirit that could overcome even the greatest kingdoms on the earth.

TURNING THE TIDE

Today, we are faced with overwhelming opposition. Even in a country like ours where so many people still

140

believe in God and call on the name of Jesus, it has become harder and harder to serve God openly. Laws are passed restricting our freedoms. We are often prohibited from evangelizing. The media elites develop interlocking ownership structures that effectively shut out Christian groups.

Our power and influence in the world has fluctuated through the centuries, and today Christians need a new strength.

It can be discouraging, to say the least, to try to make a difference. Yet I believe there are some very practical things people can undertake.

In their discussion over the sins of Sodom and Gomorrah, God told Abraham that He would spare the cities if only ten righteous people – a tiny fraction of the population at that time – repented.

Likewise today, I believe that if just one percent of the born again Christians in this country would agree to take a stand, we can make a real difference.

I have stopped counting the times people have shrugged their shoulders and lamented, "What can we do? How can we turn the tide?"

> IF JUST ONE PERCENT OF THE BORN AGAIN CHRISTIANS IN THIS COUNTRY WOULD AGREE TO TAKE A STAND, WE CAN MAKE A REAL DIFFERENCE

141

Throughout our nation I have sensed the hopelessness, even resignation, of many Christians as they watch the invasion of ungodly forces creep into their homes and lives.

> THERE IS MUCH WE CAN DO – AND IT BEGINS WITH YOU AND ME

Friend, it is not too late. There is much we can do – and it begins with you and me.

WHAT WE CAN DO?

Here are eleven essential things every Christian should do to make a difference.

1. Turn off the darkness.

It is time to change the channel for good! Make a vow to God that you will no longer allow the garbage and filth of this world to invade your home and your mind.

2. Make a covenant with your eyes.

Determine that they will become the gatekeepers of what you allow to penetrate your soul. The psalmist declared, "I will set nothing wicked before my eyes" (Psalms 101:3).

Everywhere, people are drowning in a sea of darkness, and you do not need to be pulled under. Simply turn it off – do not watch it!

Again, we need to make the pledge of the psalmist, who

wrote, "Turn away my eyes from looking at worthless things" (Psalms 119:37).

We have a choice. Will we be a part of the darkness, or will we be a part of the light? Jesus said, "Let your light so shine before men, that they may see your good works and glorify your Father in heaven" (Matthew 5:16).

Seek out those things that are pure, wholesome and of good report. Think on – and *watch* – these things.

3. Wage spiritual warfare.

The temptation is to fight this battle the wrong way. We cannot fight the world with the weapons of the world. We do not need a sword of steel. We need the sword of the spirit.

Let's face it. The devil has declared war on you and your family. As a result you need to take the spiritual offensive – not the defensive! It is time for you to get spiritually violent.

> WE CANNOT FIGHT THE WORLD WITH THE WEAPONS OF THE WORLD

Remember, the kingdom of heaven suffers violence and the violent take it by force! (Matthew 11:12).

Put on the whole armor of God. Now is the time to confront the forces of the enemy in Jesus' name. We must bind the negative evil-influencing principalities and powers that are coming against our families daily. Take authority over the spirit of sin, rebellion, lawlessness, perversion, promiscuity, and violence.

Jesus declared, "I will give you the keys of the kingdom of heaven, and whatever you bind on earth will be bound in heaven, and whatever you loose on earth will be loosed in heaven" (Matthew 16:19).

Pray that over this land there will sweep a spirit of conviction, righteousness, holiness and salvation.

4. Watch programs that are wholesome.

You have often heard the words, "You are what you eat!" These maxims are also probably true: "You are what you read!" "You are what you listen to!" And, "You are what you watch!"

> TELEVISION HAS BECOME THE MOST PERVASIVE "MESSENGER" OF ALL

Television has become perhaps the most pervasive "messenger" of all – more than radio, books, movies or music. Why? Because people spend more time in front of the television set than almost any other single function short of sleeping and work. It bombards us with messages, messages, and more messages every day.

We need to filter out anything that does not uplift or edify. And we need to monitor both the quantity and the quality of information entering our minds. Paul the Apostle wrote, "All things are lawful for me, but not all things are helpful; all things are lawful for me, but not all things edify"

(1 Corinthians 10:23).

5. Practice "lighting a candle" rather than "cursing the darkness."

It is easy to complain, yet more difficult to contribute.

When Jesus was with His disciples in the Garden of Gethsemane, He told them to "Watch and pray, lest you enter into temptation. The spirit indeed is willing, but the flesh is weak" (Matthew 26:41).

Much of the world and media leaders associate Christians with negativity. Certainly we must be outspoken when necessary, take a stand against those who promote wrong values and ungodly content, and take other appropriate actions. However, *we must learn to do positive things. Let's confront the powers of darkness with light.* Light is the only thing that can and will dispel darkness. How do we do that? By helping to produce programs that will shed the light of the gospel across the broadcast airwaves.

A law of science is that "nature abhors a vacuum." In other words, where there is a void, something will come along to fill it.

> A LAW OF SCIENCE IS THAT "NATURE ABHORS A VACUUM."

People have a genuine need for comedy, drama, music, and other family-oriented entertainment. We cannot just condemn; we must offer new choices.

145

If we only curse the darkness nothing will change. How much better to light a candle, raise a righteous standard and provide an alternative.

6. Learn to be sensitive to program content.

Pay attention to what people are saying on television, and recognize that you have the right to determine what you listen to and watch – and who will influence you and your family.

RECOGNIZE THAT YOU HAVE THE RIGHT TO DETERMINE WHAT YOU LISTEN TO AND WATCH

Examine the programs and networks that your children are viewing and take responsible steps to guide them in making wise, Godly choices.

Do not allow yourself to become desensitized. As an earlier chapter in this book detailed, far too many parents have abdicated their responsibility in this area. We have to be on guard. The values, lifestyles, beliefs and choices of our children and families are being influenced to an unprecedented degree by Satan. One of the many tools in his arsenal is television. So many television media professionals embrace values and beliefs which are often ungodly, anti-Christian and in general contrary to the word of God. Their values, rooted in darkness, manifest themselves in the programming coming into our homes.

One of the most important, and practical things Christians can do is to pay attention to the content of programs, especially programs that specifically target children.

7. Support organizations that produce, televise, and sponsor programs and networks that maintain Biblical values.

Here are four specific actions you can take:

- Make a determined effort to personally watch wholesome programs. Television is driven by ratings. Do everything in your power to increase the audience for worthwhile media.

> DO EVERYTHING IN YOUR POWER TO INCREASE THE AUDIENCE FOR WORTHWHILE MEDIA

- Write your cable company. Encourage them to drop channels that continue to bombard us with darkness and add more wholesome and uplifting channels. (This can be as easy as putting a handwritten note on your cable bill.)
- Buy the products of companies that sponsor quality programming.
- Pray for and support organizations that are

attempting to offer an alternative to the darkness on television.

These are not one-time activities. Show your support on a continuing basis.

8. Fight the influence of those who have as their agenda a society without Biblical standards.

Learn to recognize the people and companies that openly promote darkness and ungodliness and flaunt and defy Biblical values.

The way our system works is to make your opinion heard. Do not be passive, or the influence of ungodly people will continue to infiltrate your home, family, and community.

Here are things you can do:

- Have the cable system block out channels you find offensive. If that is not technically possible in your area, protest as loudly as you can. If necessary, cancel your subscription unless changes are made.
- Complain to cable companies, broadcast stations, newspapers, and others when you see something that is distasteful.

9. Lobby political leaders to force broadcasters, cable systems, and programmers to take responsibility for their actions.

I am not advocating full-scale government censorship. However, if we love God, our country and our children – and desire a brighter future – we need to let our leaders know that we expect them to make those responsible for communications in our country accountable for their actions.

Obtain the names and addresses of your congressmen, senators and representatives. Communicate with them regularly for ethical and reputable programming.

10. Pray for God to send revival to our land.

Believe that "the earth will be filled with the knowledge of the glory of the Lord, As the waters cover the sea" (Habakkuk 2:14).

God can bring about change, but His people need to be a praying people. It gives us focus and direction. We need to:

> GOD CAN BRING ABOUT CHANGE, BUT HIS PEOPLE NEED TO BE A PRAYING PEOPLE

Pray for ourselves:

Lord, help us think about what is right, pure, lovely, admirable, excellent, and praiseworthy. May the words of our lips and the meditations of our heart be acceptable to You. May all we do in thought, word, and deed, bring You glory.

Pray for our leaders:

God, bless the leaders of our country and give them wisdom. May they come to know and serve You. Let them lead our country with righteousness. Give them the boldness to do what is right, and to take a stand for honor and truth.

Pray for the communications industry:
Heavenly Father, bring about the end of the influence of the prince of the powers of the air. Draw the men and women in leadership in television, the film industry, the Internet, direct broadcast satellite companies, and other communications media to You. Give boldness and favor to the ones who desire to take a stand for You and Godly principles.

11. Help us at INSP as we attempt to create a new kind of television network that maintains Biblical and Christ-centered values.

The desire of my heart is to birth a new kind of network that includes programs of the highest production standards. People should not be expected to watch television today unless it maintains these standards.

This network will have programs that are entertaining, informative, and engaging – for every member of the family. Most importantly this programming will be inspiring and redemptive.

We will maintain Biblical values and will never promote anything that is contrary to Christianity or the word of God. We are trying to make The Inspirational Networks a blend of the best in teaching and preaching programs complimented by the best in Christ-centered, entertaining and redemptive programs for the entire family.

We cannot undertake such a task alone. Our desire is to continue to work with other organizations, denominations, producers and writers to form strategic alliances and partnerships.

God has given us a vision to change the world for good, one life at a time, through television – a vision to positively impact people's values, beliefs, behavior and most importantly their relationship to God, their family and their fellow man. "And this we will do if God permits" (Hebrews 6:3).

> "AND THIS WE WILL DO IF GOD PERMITS."
> – *HEBREWS 6:3*

My prayer is that people throughout America and the world will join with us in this unique effort.

IT BEGINS WITH YOU

The challenge looming on the horizon is enormous, and there are many times when I understand just how the spies felt when they returned from the Promised Land (Numbers 13:1-33).

They had heard the promises of great potential, how the fruit was large and the opportunities were great. Yet when they entered the land, they realized it was occupied – and not by ordinary people. It was filled with giants!

While these leaders of Israel once felt confident and

151

strong, after seeing the giants they now "seemed like grass-hoppers."

They responded to the enormity of the challenge with fear, discouragement, and defeatism. They had forgotten the God who parted the seas, who brought forth water from the rock, and lead them by a pillar of fire by day and a cloud by night.

The children of Israel became a downcast people who expected defeat and rejected the power, authority, and even the ability of God. The Psalmist recorded these words: "Today, if you will hear His voice: Do not harden your hearts, as in the rebellion, As in the day of trial in the wilderness, When your fathers tested Me; They tried Me, though they saw My work. For forty years I was grieved with that generation, And said, 'It is a people who go astray in their hearts, And they do not know My ways.' So I swore in My wrath, 'They shall not enter My rest'" (Psalms 95:7-11).

> **WE MOST FOLLOW OUR BELIEF WITH DEEDS AND COMBINE OUR FAITH WITH ACTION**

To enter into God's rest, to possess the land, to receive God's blessing, we must move forward with boldness and confidence. Perhaps our task is to start with an awareness of how critical things truly are, and the obstacles we face.

The Bible makes it clear that we must follow our belief with deeds and combine our faith with action. James wrote, "Show me your faith without deeds, and I will show you my faith by what I do" (James 2:8).

Today, we need Christians who will proclaim their faith by their actions – and follow up their words with deeds.

Will you join me in turning off the darkness? Together, we can change the world for good!

Resources

Chapter 1

1. *Violence and Youth* (Washington, D.C: American Psychological Association, 1993).

2. Report by the American Academy of Pediatrics, May, 1999.

3. Jeffery Mortimer, "How Violence Hits Kids," *The Education Digest*, October, 1994, p.16.

4. Orrin Hatch, quoted in Darlene Superville, Associated Press, "Report: Media Violence Affects Kids," Internet: www.washingtonpost.com, August 6, 1999.

5. Darlene Superville, Associated Press, "Report: Media Violence Affects Kids," Internet: www.washingtonpost.com, August 6, 1999.

6. Michael Medved, *Hollywood Vs. America* (New York: HarperCollins, 1993), p. 183.

7. Kathryn Montgomery, quoted in "Children, Media and Violence," *New York Times*, May 9, 1999.

8. "U.S. TV Programs 'More Lewd' Than Ever," *Reuters News*, September 1, 1999

9. Thomas Storke, Testimony at U.S. Senate Hearings on "The Social Impact of Music Violence," November 6, 1977.

10. "Violence and Media," *Reuters News*, May 14, 1997.

11. Reported in *Archives of Pediatrics and Adolescent Medicine*, May 1997.

Chapter 2

1. "Religion in America: Report in The Public Perspective," The Gallup Organization, Vol. 6, No. 6, Oct./Nov., 1995.
2. The U.S. News & World Report, Internet: www.usnews.com, May 12, 1999.
3. Quoted in Robin Brown, "Bozell Group: TV Raunch is Words Despite Ratings," Hollywood Reporter, May 27, 1999.
4. The Gallup Organization, Internet, www.gallup.com, June 3, 1999.
5. "Communicating Family Values," Massachusetts Mutual Insurance Company, 1992.
6. The Gallup Organization, Princeton, NJ. Internet: www. gallup.com, July 2, 1999.

Chapter 3

1. Quoted in Michael Medved, *Hollywood Vs. America* (New York: HarperCollins, 1992), p.71.
2. Ibid., p.79.
3. Tim LaHaye, *The Hidden Censors* (Old Tappan, NJ: Fleming H. Revell, 1984), p.3.
4. "Tabloid TV is Bad News for Kids," Washington, D.C.: Center for Media and Public Affairs, December 22, 1997.
5. Michael Medved, *Hollywood Vs. America* (New York:HarperCollins, 1992), p.33.
6. Ibid., p.3.

7. MovieGuide is available through the Internet at http://movieguide.crosswalk.com.

Chapter 4

1. "WWF Move Causes Death of Three year Old Boy," Internet, http://dallas.about.com. September 2, 1999.
2. William Cockburn, "Video Games – A Note of Caution." www.parenthoodweb.com, August 8, 1999.
3. "Children and TV Violency," American Academy of Child and Adolescent Psychiatry, www.parenthoodweb.com, August 8, 1999.
4. "Pediatricians Suggest Limits on TV," Washington Post, August 4, 1999. Internet: search.washingtonpost.com.

Chapter 6

1. "List of Multiple Shootings This Year," Associated Press, August 10, 1999.
2. Report on study by Parents Television Council, *Hollywood Reporter*, May 27, 1999.

About the Author

DAVID CERULLO has been the President and Chief Executive Officer of The Inspirational Networks since 1990. As of this writing, The Inspirational Networks are comprised of three different networks: The Inspirational Network, Inspirational Life and Inspirational Education. Headquarters are in Charlotte, North Carolina.

David has been an ordained minister of the gospel for over 25 years. However, he considers his calling more in the realm of business and administration than a pulpit or speaking ministry.

He has a wide-ranging national and international background, including extensive travel throughout Europe, Latin America, Africa and Asia where he has organized numerous projects in both ministry and business.

David is a graduate of Oral Roberts University, with a degree in Business Administration and Management and holds numerous credentials from various continuing educational organizations including American Management Association, Annual and Deferred Gifts Institutes, Philanthropy Tax Institute, and others. He is a member of outstanding Young Men of America, NCTA (National Cable Television Association), CTAM, (Cable and Telecommunications Association for Marketing), an associate member of NATPE International (National Association of Television Program Executives), and serves on the Board of Directors for the NRB (the National Religious Broadcasters Association) as well as his father's ministry, Morris Cerullo World Evangelism.

He has diverse and extensive experience in international ministry, real estate development, construction project administration and all aspects of cable network programming and management.

David and his wife, Barbara, are the parents of two adult children, Ben and Becky; both are married.